Balancing Islamic and Conventional Banking for Economic Growth

Murat Ustaoğlu · Ahmet İncekara
Editors

Balancing Islamic and Conventional Banking for Economic Growth

Empirical Evidence from Emerging Economies

palgrave
macmillan

Editors
Murat Ustaoğlu
Istanbul University
Istanbul, Turkey

Ahmet İncekara
Istanbul University
Istanbul, Turkey

ISBN 978-3-319-59553-5 ISBN 978-3-319-59554-2 (eBook)
DOI 10.1007/978-3-319-59554-2

Library of Congress Control Number:2017944098

Printed on acid-free paper

This Palgrave Macmillan imprint is published by Springer Nature
The registered company is Springer International Publishing AG
The registered company address is: Gewerbestrasse 11, 6330 Cham, Switzerland

Spread wheat on mountains so that people would not speculate that birds starve in the lands of Muslims.

Umar ibn Al-Khattāb,
The Second Khalif

To my mentor Muharrem Balcı, Esq

Preface

The regulation and institutionalization of the borrowing transactions has been done only a few centuries ago. The sector that first emerged in the West has spread all over the world in a way to meet the financial needs of the real sectors, also contributing to the development and growth. A small margin in the growth rate leads to dramatic gaps between the welfares of the nations. For this reason, growth is extremely crucial for a society to keep its prosperity. Economists focusing on this issue have investigated the dynamics to analyse the impact of technological developments upon growth. It is unrealistic to expect that an economy where technology fails to provide sufficient contribution will attain stability in the long run. Technological development depends upon promotion of new investments. The financial markets are now growing fast due to the advanced technology used in communication. The financial system provides the funds for the investment projects needed for further development.

Particularly the studies analysing the developments after industrial revolution are focused on the contribution by the financial markets to the physical capital stock because the technological investments affecting the efficiency of the production factors can be made through financial capital. For this reason, in an economy where the financial markets do not operate well, a productive and competitive real sector cannot be expected. In a well-operating financial market, the borrowing transactions are also competitive because the interest rate is determined theoretically by the balance between supply and demand of the loan in a free market. At the optimum equilibrium, if the financial resources are used wisely, the physical capital stock increases and makes contribution to the competitiveness of the economy.

The importance of the financial sector becomes clear when all the sectors are affected by the malfunction of the system. At times when proper solutions are not offered, the problems turn into structural flaws, taking the economy to deeper crises. For this reason, the relevant institutions, monitoring the economic developments, take measures to regulate the system. A quick look at the history of economy in the world tells us that the adequacy of the conventional measures remains controversial. It is not possible to argue that the interest-based conventional measures have worked well to resolve the economic issues. Major crises still emerge, affecting the lives of billions all around the world and exacerbating the global poverty. Despite this, nothing has been done to offer an alternative up until recent decades.

The global crisis in the American financial markets in 2008 has deeply affected the world. On the other hand, the good performance of the Islamic finance has attracted attention during the crisis. For this reason, it has become a major discussion in the Muslim world and the Western countries. The debates in the Muslim countries (most of which are developing nations) have been focused on a wide range of issues including the legal status of Islamic finance and the managerial performance.

Some Muslim scholars argue that Islamic finance is nothing more than a slightly different version of the interest-based conventional system; but those who subscribe to a moderate view are of the opinion that it is a promising alternative financial model that may contribute to addressing the gap between the Muslim world and the modern developed world. Both approaches offer solid arguments; the first group of scholars refers to the technical details in the Islamic law because the Islamic financial institutions in the different parts of the world have to comply with the rules of a secular legal system. This often leads to complexities and issues because of the detailed approaches employed in Islamic law.

Obviously, a financial system that does not make any major difference cannot be expected to serve as an alternative. For this reason, the ability of the Islamic finance to hold its potential of serving as an alternative depends upon its capability of growing further and proving its success in the markets. A moral alternative can be offered only if its remains attached to the main precepts of Islam. For this reason, it has to observe major priorities including protection of the environment, loss- and profit-sharing and a balanced approach to the markets.

If these main principles are eroded, it will eventually lose its popularity and assertion of becoming an alternative to the conventional model even if it is still successful in terms of contribution to development and real sector. This has to remain one of the priorities of the sector in different parts of the world. Given that major breakthroughs have been performed in the Western world and that the Muslim nations have remained mere bystanders, the importance of a successful Islamic finance becomes clear. In case of stable success, the Islamic finance may become the global brand of Islam. One of the goals of this study is to contribute to this process.

Istanbul, Turkey, 2017

Dr. Murat Ustaoğlu

Acknowledgements

Authors would like to thank *Dr. Halis Yunus Ersöz, Marwah Maasarani, Ahmet Buğra Aydın, Zehra Betül Ustaoğlu, Sadri Özturan, Semih Boybay, Serkan Kırkyaşaroğlu, Bilal Cantaş, Mustafa Atas and Ayhan Sağır* for their contributions to this research.

The authors also offer special thanks to *Dr. Cenap Çakmak* who has spent a great deal of time and effort on this research, the process would not have been completed without his valuable assistance.

Additionally, appreciate and recognize the *Istanbul University Scientific Research Projects Department's* financial support.

Contents

Editors and Contributors

About the Editors

Dr. Murat Ustaoğlu is an Associate Professor of Islamic Economics. He was born in Turkey, and educated at the Ramapo College of New Jersey (B.A.) and the City University of New York (M.A.), and holds a Ph.D. degree in Economics. Dr. Ustaoğlu has worked at Bank of New York and JP Morgan Chase Bank in US. He is, most recently, co-author of Islamic Finance Alternatives for Emerging Economies (2014), Post-Conflict Syrian State and Nation Building (2015) and many research articles focusing Islamic Finance and Economics. Additionally, he teaches undergraduate and graduate level various courses in Economics.

Dr. Ahmet İncekara is a Professor of Economics at the Istanbul University and Head of the Department of Economics. He was born and educated in Turkey, and has taught various courses in there. Prof. İncekara has published many books including Islamic Finance Alternatives for Emerging Economies (2014), and research articles in the field of Economics. He is also head of the Economic Research Foundation in İstanbul since 2009.

Contributors

Mehmet Akyol Istanbul University, Istanbul, Turkey

Servet Bayındır Istanbul University, Istanbul, Turkey

Selim Demez Istanbul University, Istanbul, Turkey

Elif Haykır Hobikoğlu Istanbul University, Istanbul, Turkey

Hülya Deniz Karakoyun Istanbul University, Istanbul, Turkey

Zeynep Karaçor Selçuk University, Konya, Turkey

Adem Levent Istanbul University, Istanbul, Turkey

Halil Şimşek University of Toronto, Toronto, ON, Canada

Ferda Yerdelen Tatoğlu Istanbul University, Istanbul, Turkey

Halil Tunalı Istanbul University, Istanbul, Turkey

Selman Yılmaz Istanbul University, Istanbul, Turkey

List of Tables

CHAPTER 1

Introduction

Ahmet İncekara and Murat Ustaoğlu

Abstract Economics, as a social science, is a discipline that seeks to ensure a sound relationship between man and the universe, paying attention to human factor the most. It relies on the assumption that man will become happy when he attains greater prosperity and seeks to ensure that every individual improves their lifestyle by utilizing a variety of instruments. For this reason, many countries made efforts to implement the most appropriate policies in order to improve social welfare standards. The primary objective of these policies is to attain reasonable growth rates that are considered to be indicators of welfare level. Despite some opposing views, real sector is considered the main engine for a good growth performance. This study analyses the relationship between finance and growth in selected Islamic countries using empirical findings.

Keywords Dual banking · Islamic finance · Economic growth

A. İncekara (✉) · M. Ustaoğlu
Istanbul University, Istanbul, Turkey
e-mail: incekara@istanbul.edu.tr

M. Ustaoğlu
e-mail: ustaoglu@istanbul.edu.tr

M. Ustaoğlu and A. İncekara (eds.), *Balancing Islamic and Conventional Banking for Economic Growth*, DOI 10.1007/978-3-319-59554-2_1

Introduction

The Western world has accomplished a dramatic economic transformation over the past centuries thanks to the industrial revolution. Advances in science and technology have led to radical changes in production techniques and increases in demands for goods and services. This eventually contributed enormously to the welfare level (Ali et al. 2014). Many countries have developed new methods to ensure real increase and surplus in the production of goods and services. The states which were able to adapt the technological and scientific inventions to production have attained high growth rates. Economists call the real increase and performance in the goods and services growth, which becomes a major factor in a number of fields including economic transactions, interstate relations and political engagements. Even a small margin in the growth rates of two countries can cause a huge gap in terms of development levels in the long term (Pamuk 2015). For this reason, almost every country is focused on economic policies that seek to ensure the highest possible growth rate. A review of the developed nations indicates that sectors such as automotive, petrochemical industry, electrical vehicles and vessel construction make the greatest contribution to the growth. Additionally, agriculture, mining, construction and tourism also seem to be popular sectors for good growth performance.

Real sector is considered the main engine of growth; but empirical studies also show that an advanced financial sector is also important. A well functioning financial system channels savings to the economy, ensuring that these resources are used to fund economic activities (Lai 2015). A number of economists believe that the foundations of the modern economy have been laid down by the establishment of the modern banking system (Ferguson 2015). Modern banking provides finance to the capital used in the production and thus contributes to the development of production systems. The spread of new technologies and realization of capital accumulation requires availability of funds; for this reason, an advanced financial system is an important element to the process of growth, because they are able to channel the small amount of savings to huge investments (Bangake and Eggoh 2011). Additionally, they ensure diversification of investments and thus minimize the risks for investors and savings holders. Thanks to the technical opportunities and expertise, they can exhibit a better performance in the investment projects. As a result, they can immensely contribute to growth and high rate of productivity (Aslan and Küçükaksoy 2006). This indicates that sustainable growth requires good financial performance. However, despite this commonly held agreement that a strong financial system is an important element in the economic system, there is no consensus as to how financial performance is measured. Some economists refer to total market capitalization and market transaction volume whereas others look at the ratio of total loans and total savings of the national income for a better understanding of financial development and performance. One issue that economists grapple with is the relationship between finance and growth.

Studies on the direction of and relationship between finance and growth can be evaluated based on four main assumptions. The first group of theories argues that growth leads to financial development, and suggests that growth takes place first, being followed by the development of a financial system that supplies funds. According to this approach, growth fosters the financial sector. The second popular approach in the literature argues that the relationship runs just the opposite. This theory indicates that the development of financial markets takes place before growth, for this reason, financial system contributes to growth. The financial sector accelerates the process of inclusion of savings in the economy. The easy access to funds becomes an advantage in terms of competition which then also contributes to the increased amount of consumption. For this reason, the direction of the relationship is from the development of a financial sector to growth. The third theory, on the other hand, indicates that there is a mutual relationship between financial development and growth. This approach stresses that when growth slows down, the financial sector is affected; and if the financial sector experiences difficulties, this will also have an impact on economic performance. A fourth approach claims that there is no linkage between financial development and growth, suggesting that the two are independent from each other (Kandır 2007). It is possible to refer to studies in the literature supporting each one of these four approaches. The findings in this study support the argument that there is a mutual relationship between the two.

The diversity in the views on the direction of the relationship does not change the fact that a sound financial system provides funds for sustainable development. For this reason, an improved financial system remains important for stable growth. In some Islamic countries, the financial system is composed of two elements: conventional financial system (CF) and Islamic financial system (IF). Thanks to the privileges associated with the IF, the financial options and opportunities are greater in some Islamic countries including Turkey, Malaysia, Indonesia and Qatar. The IF, relatively very new compared to the CF, offers better options in terms of meeting the financial needs of the real sector (Yanpar 2015). The IF, by definition, has to use the funds it collects from the saving holders in trade-related activities (Beck et al. 2013). The profits they make mostly rely on the partnership models realized through real sector projects in line with the philosophy and idea that serves as the foundation of their presence. To better understand the importance of this structural feature of the IF, it is sufficient to evaluate the performance of the IF institutions during the global financial crisis (Lai 2015). The roots of the crisis that negatively affected world economy can be attributed to the selfish and irresponsible practices of the CF (Beck 2014). Due to these practices, some CF institutions faced bankruptcy; however, in the same period, the IF institutions have increased their assets by 28.6 *pct*. This gives an idea on the difference between the two systems (Yanpar 2015). The selfish and irresponsible practices of the CF which pay no attention to public utility have taken the global economy to the edge of collapse.

In fact, the IF owes its popularity to the flaws of the CF and the public reactions to the poor performance of the conventional banking institutions. The placard that appeared during the Occupy Wall Street protests which reads, 'Let's bank Islamic way', is an interesting example signifying this public reaction. For the first time, part of the Western world started to discuss whether or not a religious alternative financial model can save the capitalist system (Irfan 2014). Time will show whether or not the IF saves the capitalist world; but its contribution to the real economy, its solid performance during the crises and the steady growth it has attained in the past decades indicate that it will remain popular for the foreseeable future (Bhuiyan 2015). The most important distinction between the IF and the CF is its philosophy and principles which do not comply with the capitalist assumptions and prepositions. Yanpar (2015) holds that this system, based on the Islamic rules and ethical values, may serve as a guide if the world shows courage to create a new financial system in the future.

The contribution of the capitalist Western world to the current level of global welfare cannot be underestimated. Despite the weakened image after the crisis in 2008, the financial system still remains the main force in the development of the West (Ferguson 2015). Aware of this reality, developing Islamic nations including Turkey, Malaysia and Indonesia have designed their economic policies in line with the development policies implemented in the West. These nations, trying to act in line with the popular trend in the world, have sought to use the utilities of the interest-based conventional system for financing growth (Bordo and Rousseau 2012). On the other hand, reliance on interest in the construction and operation of the financial system has caused some theological problems in Islamic nations due to the strong religious prohibition in the Abrahamic religions on interest. Islam seems to be the only religion that places the greatest emphasis upon this ban in modern times. To overcome this problem, some attempts have been made in Islamic countries. And the most concrete step was first taken in 1973 when the Islamic Development Bank was established. This paved the way for the institutionalization of IF. The main idea was to attract petro-dollars to the Islamic countries and to ensure involvement of Muslim individuals in the mainstream economy. But the most distinctive characteristic of the IF is its reliance on interest-free model in the financial transactions. However, whether or not these institutions truly rely on interest-free instruments remains controversial.

Some economists and theologians argue that this argument is baseless. The whole argument is based on the idea that there are no significant differences between IF products and those of the CF. But those who hold optimistic views suggest that despite some of its mistakes, the IF remains in line with the main precepts of Islamic law in its operations and practices. Yet it would be realistic to say that not all reservations or concerns have been addressed so far. The study can be justified by the diversity of the views on the compatibility of the IF activities with the Islamic rules and precepts. It should be noted, however, that the theological dimension of the IF activities is not part of this research.

Before empirical chapters that comparatively analyse the financing of growth in some Muslim countries, it is necessary to take a look at the evolution of the Islamic finance for a better understanding. For this reason, the first two chapters are dedicated to the evolution and progress of the IF since the 1970s, followed by an evaluation of the common problems that the IF encounters in the world. The introductory section also deals with the main features and principles of the IF. Subsequently, this section also analyses the practices and policies pursued in different sectors in Turkey, Malaysia, Indonesia and Qatar.

Chapters from 3 to 7 focus on the relationship between finance and growth through empirical analyses. First, the main concepts that will help understand this linkage are explained. The theories presented in the literature on the direction of the relationship in the short and long terms are evaluated in great detail. Additionally, the empirical findings in the study are also evaluated. This chapter serves as the theoretical background and literature review of the whole research. The roles and functions of the CF and IF on the growth are comparatively analysed to better measure the contributions of the financial institutions to growth in Turkey, Malaysia, Indonesia and Qatar.

Chapter 4 investigates the development policies, the dynamics of the domestic policies and the economic policies implemented in Turkey. The chapter explains the structural transformation from the Ottoman era to the republican period and further measures the performance of the financial practices and mechanisms in this period. The importance of the CF and IF in the national economy is evaluated. Subsequently, the chapter empirically measures the contribution of the financial sector to the growth in agriculture, mining, manufacturing, construction and tourism.

Chapter 5 analyses the economic policies of Malaysia, considered one of the most important economies in the Far East and the Muslim world in general. Further, it reviews the policies implemented for the growth of agriculture, manufacturing, tourism and construction sectors. The funds provided to real sector are comparatively analysed and the growth performance of the sectors is also benchmarked based on empirical findings and evidence. Chapter 6 focuses on Indonesia and its economic performance since its independence. The structural transformation is explained in this chapter. The economic dynamics of the sectors reviewed are analysed and the performance of the CF and IF in the development of the sectors is measured empirically. Chapter 8 focuses on the economic development of Qatar, a major oil exporting country in the Gulf, and analyses the growth dynamics and economic policies implemented in this country. The chapter further analyses the impact of the loans provided by the dual banking system upon growth and the sectors reviewed in the study.

The purpose of this study is to offer a comparative benchmark of how growth is financed in selected Islamic countries. For this reason, some criteria have been taken into consideration in the selection of the countries included in the analysis. The first criterion is that the country to be included should be a developing Islamic nation. The second criterion suggests that this country should have a dual banking system (both IF and CF). Without a dual banking system, a comparative analysis cannot be offered. For this reason, Pakistan, Iran and Saudi Arabia were excluded. The final criterion is the availability of the information on the loans provided by the financial system for the sectors. This information has been collected from the central bank and statistical offices of each country. The data have been included in the econometric model. Because it was not possible to have access to the data provided by Egypt, Jordan and United Arab Emirates, these countries were not included in the scope of the research. Similar sectors and dataset covering same period have been used in this study.

References

Ali, S.N., U.A. Oseni, and S. Nisar. 2014. *Islamic finance and development*, vol. viii, 314. Cambridge, MA: Islamic Finance Project, Islamic Legal Studies Program, Harvard Law School.

Aslan, Ö., and İ. Küçükaksoy. 2006. Finansal gelişme ve ekonomik büyüme ilişkisi: Türkiye ekonomisi üzerine ekonometrik bir uygulama. *Ekonometri ve İstatistik* 4 (1): 12–28.

Bangake, C., and J.C. Eggoh. 2011. Further evidence on finance-growth causality: A panel data analysis. *Economic Systems* 35 (2): 176–188.

Beck, T. 2014. Finance, growth, and stability: Lessons from the crisis. *Journal of Financial Stability* 10 (1): 1–6.

Beck, T., A. Demirguc-Kunt, and O. Merrouche. 2013. Islamic vs. Conventional banking: Business model, efficiency and stability. *Journal of Banking & Finance* 37 (2): 433–447.

Bhuiyan, R.A. 2015. Fundamentals of Islamic banking. *International Journal of Economics Management and Accounting* 23 (2): 271–273.

Bordo, M.D., and P.L. Rousseau. 2012. Historical evidence on the finance-trade-growth nexus. *Journal of Banking & Finance* 36 (4): 1236–1243.

Ferguson, N. 2015. *Paranın Yükselişi: Dünyanın Finansal Tarihi*. ed. Baskı, 3. İstanbul: Yapı Kredi Yayınları.

Irfan, H. 2014. Could Islamic finance save capitalism? In *The Guardian*, 11. London. https://www.theguardian.com/sustainable-business/2014/dec/04/could-islamic-finance-solution-capitalism.

Kandır, S.Y., Ö. İskenderoğlu, and Y.B. Önal. 2007. Finansal gelişme ve ekonomik büyüme arasındaki ilişkinin araştırılması. *Ç.Ü. Sosyal Bilimler Enstitüsü Dergisi* 16 (2): 311–326.

Lai, J. 2015. Industrial policy and Islamic finance. *New Political Economy* 20 (2): 178–198.

Pamuk, Ş. 2015. *Türkiye'nin 200 Yıllık İktisadi Tarihi*, 377. İstanbul: Türkiye İş Bankası Kültür Yayınları.

Yanpar, A. 2015. *İslami Finans: İlkeler, Araçlar ve Kurumlar*. İstanbul: Scala Yayıncılık.

Authors' Biography

Dr. Ahmet İncekara is a Professor of Economics at the Istanbul University and Head of the Department of Economics. He was born and educated in Turkey, and has taught various courses in there. Prof. İncekara has published many books including Islamic Finance Alternatives for Emerging Economies (2014), and research articles in the field of Economics. He is also head of the Economic Research Foundation in İstanbul since 2009.

Dr. Murat Ustaoğlu is an Associate Professor of Islamic Economics. He was born in Turkey, and educated at the Ramapo College of New Jersey (B.A.) and the City University of New York (M.A.), and holds a Ph.D. degree in Economics. Dr. Ustaoğlu has worked at Bank of New York and JP Morgan Chase Bank in US. He is, most recently, co-author of Islamic Finance Alternatives for Emerging Economies (2014), Post-Conflict Syrian State and Nation Building (2015) and many research articles focusing Islamic Finance and Economics. Additionally, he teaches undergraduate and graduate level various courses in Economics.

CHAPTER 2

Dual Banking Systems' Dynamics and a Brief Development History of Islamic Finance in Select Emerging Islamic Economies

Halil Şimşek, Servet Bayındır and Murat Ustaoğlu

Abstract Major religions in the world have introduced an interest ban for different reasons. Those other than Islam have, however, made lenient changes to this ban over the centuries, ultimately completely eliminating it. As a result, the modern financial system has evolved onto the interest-based banking model which played a huge role in the development of the Western world. On the other hand, most Muslims have distanced themselves to this model for religious reasons in predominantly

H. Şimşek
University of Toronto, Toronto, ON, Canada
e-mail: h.simsek@utoronto.ca

S. Bayındır (✉)
Istanbul University, Istanbul, Turkey
e-mail: servetbayindir@hotmail.com

M. Ustaoğlu
Istanbul University, Istanbul, Turkey
e-mail: ustaoglu@istanbul.edu.tr

M. Ustaoğlu and A. İncekara (eds.), *Balancing Islamic and Conventional Banking for Economic Growth*, DOI 10.1007/978-3-319-59554-2_2

Muslim countries, leaving most financial sources idle. As a cure to this problem, an alternative model based on PLS principle has been offered, briefly called Islamic Finance (IF). A dual banking system has subsequently emerged with the involvement of both conventional and Islamic finance models in the system in some countries in the world.

Keywords Dual banking · Islamic finance · Emerging economies

Introduction

Economic relations which took two forms of monetary and real foundations reveal themselves in the measurement of the performance in improving the welfare of the people in the growth process. Harmony between real and financial sectors in the economy is very important. The main function of the financial sector in the growth process is to ensure that the real production increases are involved in the process of reproduction. And this becomes possible in case of a financial structure that is well organized and well functioning (Nişancı et al. 2011). For this reason, a well-functioning financial system is crucially important. In this relationship, the function of the real sector can be defined as provision of high level of contribution to the national welfare through investments that improve competitiveness in global markets.

Harmony between the two sectors made positive contribution to the development process in the Western economies. With the emergence of the modern banking system, the developmental gap between the most developed and least developed areas has become a more serious concern. The financial model that contributed to this process was interest-based banking system which raised serious controversies throughout the history. In the Muslim world, on the other hand, the interest-based banking model has been discouraged because of the strong ban introduced by Islam. Even though 'monetary foundations' have been put in place in some rare occasions, no alternative model has been offered up to the 1970s. But the ground has become appropriate for an IF model in this period where debates on development have been made more frequently. It is possible to argue that the modern IF model merged the traditional commercial methods of Islam and the CF system's institutions and products.

The establishment of the Islamic banks has been followed by the emergence of Takaful (Islamic insurance) and Islamic capital market tools. In the 1950s, a group of Pakistani economists and financial experts worked on Islamic financial methods which culminated in the establishment of the first collective bank in the western part of Pakistan in 1958 (Türker 2010). In the same period, another initiative was put in place to lay the groundwork of the IF in Mit Gamr in Egypt. This was a bank based on a unique approach mixing venture-capital and monetary foundation to meet the needs of the Egyptian rural people. Developed by Dr. Ahmad Al-Naggar, this model offered a number of services including commercial partnership and insurance. The model, allegedly inspired by the social development banking in the economic history of Germany, sought to merge the economic and cultural elements of Islam as well as the contemporary trends.[1]

With the exception of some individual initiatives, the IF was first implemented in an organized method during the reign of Saudi King Faisal. A substantial amount of funds has been accumulated in the oil-producing Middle Eastern countries due to the increasing oil prices in 1970s. The accumulated monies were used to provide funds for the development policies of the Muslim countries. To materialize this idea, a huge regional bank was created. The Islamic Development Bank, founded in Jeddah in 1975, provided funds for public projects but failed to meet the finance needs of the real sector. To fill the void, a holding, Dar al Maal al Islami was established in 1981. Dallah Baraka Group, imitating this initiative and its know-how experience, developed the interest-free financial system which has spread through different Muslim countries since then.

Currently, a number of countries including non-Muslim ones spend efforts to make legislations for proper operation of the IF. Particularly in addition to Muslim countries including Gulf countries, Turkey, Malaysia and Indonesia, the US, Britain, Switzerland, Germany, Luxembourg and Canada offer incentives for IF investments in an attempt to meet the needs of the Muslim populations in their territories. Today, the total sum of the IF funds in the entire world is estimated to be around 2 trillion USD.

This part of the research deals with the meaning of the dual banking concept in the literature, followed by the evolution of the system in the Muslim world, a discussion of the criticisms directed against the system and some common problems. Subsequently, the paper research examines the evolution of the IF system in Turkey, Malaysia, Indonesia and Qatar.

Dual Banking and Islamic Finance in Global Economy

The dual banking notion was first used in the federal states of the Western world to connote subjection of banks operating in multiple provinces to both the provincial and the federal administration (Redford 1966). In the Islamic Finance literature, on the other hand, the concept refers to the presence of two different financial models in the financial sectors, particularly after the emergence of the IF as an alternative model to the conventional banking. CF, one leg of the concept, refers to the system of financial institutions mediating for the exchange of all interest-based financial products. IF, on the other hand, is a banking system that complies with the Shariah principles in the conduct of the operations performed by the CF. The model is based on the principle of removing interest in all financial transactions and processes. Capital cannot be lent without being purified from interest. In this sense, it is considered as the opposite of the modern banking system which permits profit based on money-lending.

There are some major differences between the IF and the CF. Unlike CF, there is no banker–customer relationship in the IF system. Due to the ban over all interest-based financial transactions, there is a partnership relationship based on the share of profit and loss associated with the investment. Because the fund lent for the investment has to be based on an asset, the IF institution will have to act like an investor rather than a financial lender. Additionally, under Islamic law, a contract is considered valid and binding only if such elements as subject, price and delivery time are clearly indicated. When these conditions are enforced, the IF eliminates the possibility of speculation in the financial transactions, a major setback in the CF system (Kasaroğlu 2015). The IF institutions active in the sector include commercial banks, finance companies, merchants' banks, Takaful companies, securities firms, savings institutions, rural cooperative banks, Islamic Money Market and Islamic Capital Market. But interest-free banks (participation banks) are the most effective structures and institutions of this model (Bulut 2012). Another distinction between Islamic banks and conventional counterparts is that Islamic banking does not allow involvement in a number of sectors including trade of alcohol and pornography as they are also banned in Islam. Given that these products are mostly considered harmful to the social harmony, it is possible to argue that IF enjoys a moral ground.

The countries where IF operates can be divided into two groups. The first group of countries like Iran, at least in theory, where all banks are required to comply with the Islamic rules and therefore interest-based transactions, are forbidden. The financial system of these countries is being criticized because it allegedly follows the path of the CF. The second group of countries includes Malaysia, Indonesia, United Arab Emirates, Yemen, Bangladesh, Jordan and Turkey where both interest-free and interest-based products are offered in the financial system. The dual banking system in these countries creates an advantage of competitiveness and contributes to the emergence of institutional financial structures in different fields.

The role and position of the CF in the 2008 global crisis was strongly criticized (Beck et al. 2013). On the other hand, the peculiarity of the IF financial modelling was first noticed in this crisis.[2] Even Vatican, holding the conventional banks responsible for the crisis, recommended interest-free banking as a remedy for the greatest crisis of the twenty-first century. The IF model was distinguished from its counterparts because it did not involve troubled asset, it had to make investment in real sector alone, did not pay any attention to sectors that may raise moral issues and did not allow high-risk transactions and speculations (Aras and Öztürk 2011).

Criticisms Against Islamic Finance and Some Common Problems

Despite its popularity, the IF did not attract huge attention until mid-2000s mostly because of the popular perception of the IF activities and operations. Experience shows that in cases where there is legal infrastructure, the IF flourishes. For this reason, the course of action for the IF system is obvious; the most important thing to do was to focus on policies for greater effectiveness and for removal of the ambiguities surrounding the Islamic banking. Introduction of a legal framework for the activities of a bank will inevitably improve its performance (Ergeç et al. 2014). The rapid implementation of the measures offered for the identified problems makes the IF more endurable and resistant to the cases of crisis.

While it becomes more popular, the IF also attracts criticisms for resemblance with the CF system. The criticisms are mostly based on the argument that there are extreme similarities between products offered by the IF and the CF. The small share of the partnership transactions in the financial asset portfolio reveals a tendency from risk sharing towards risk transfer (Askari et al. 2012). The flexibility in the main principles to ensure competitiveness through improvement of products and service quality will inevitably do harm to the main rationale that placed emphasis upon the IF as an alternative. Faisal (2016), noting that this is caused by imitation of the conventional banks, summarizes the main problems associated with the IF practices as follows:

i. *Adoption on Western finance*: The fact that London is considered a centre of the IF in the world should be seen as an irony. It appears that Western financial institutions have played determinative roles in the popularization of the IF. Currently, a number of Western conventional financial institutions also play a lead role in taking many IF instruments to markets. Reversing this will reduce the chance that the IF institutions will become more like conventional financial institutions.
ii. *Financialization's syndrome*: An important distinction between the IF and the CF is that the IF has to base its financial products on assets, thereby making a positive contribution to the real economy. A main principle of Islamic law dictates that commercial transactions should be promoted so welfare and prosperity is better distributed among the people more evenly. Use of the money in the financial markets rather than real sector will, however, have a detrimental impact on the effectiveness of the IF as a contributor to the economy.
iii. *Standardization*: A review of the history of a number of sectors in the modern economy reveals that standardization has played an important role in ensuring that the products will gain popularity in the markets. There is no different in the case of the IF; this has been a major challenge for the sector since its inception. A number of IF institutions in different parts of the world adopt a different version of the Islamic schools in their practices. Even though some differences among the scholarly views may be acceptable, huge diversity leads to emergence of an obstacle towards standardization. It is not that easy to offer a solution for a generalized application because the IF is extremely sensitive to the views of the religious authorities. Thus, it becomes hard to offer a middle ground between the IF and the secular legal systems in many parts

of the world. The global structures and domestic institutions set up to deal with this problem have not produced significant results yet.

The Basic Financing Tools of Islamic Finance

The funding mechanisms and tools of the IF include Mudaraba, Musharaqah, Murabaha, Ijara (leasing), Istisna' (postponed delivery), Qard, Selem (prepayment, delayed goods), Sukuk, Tawarruq, Wadi'ah and Wakala. Even though some of these instruments are similar to those used in the CF, most of them are peculiar to the IF. Instead of explaining all, it is useful to refer to four main principles (Kasaroğlu 2015):

i. *Mudaraba*: This is a labor–capital partnership where the financial institution offers its capital and the customer its labour in the investment. The profit out of the investment will be divided among the participants in accordance with the provisions of the contract. But unless a fault is directly attributed to the customer, the financial institution bears the costs associated with the loss. The liability of the customer is limited to time, labour and expertise.
ii. *Musharaqa*: This is a partnership where the financial institution offers capital and the customer both capital and expertise. As in the Mudaraba model, the revenue is divided in accordance with the previously established rules under the contract. The losses, on the other hand, are borne by the parties in proportionate to their capital contribution.
iii. *Murabaha*: This is a tripartite contract where the customer asks the financial institution to supply the product they need from the original supplier. The IF institution, acting in response to request by the customer, purchases the product from the supplier and then sells it to the customer under terms it will decide upon in installments. It should be noted that in this type of transaction, the customer is aware of the cost of the product purchased from the original supplier; and the profit margin of the IF institution is determined after talks with the customer. The total amount is paid by the customer in installments.
iv. *Ijara*: In broadest sense, this is a leasing agreement concluded in accordance with the Islamic law. In other words, under the agreement, the user is entitled to use the product. It is mostly utilized in Sukuk, the most common derivative of the IF system.

Almost all conventional financial products and services may be offered in a form of alternatives in the IF model. According to Beck, Demirgüç-Kunt who empirically reviewed the operational activities of the IF, there is a little significant difference between the IF institutions and the conventional counterparts in terms of business orientation, cost efficiency, asset quality and stability. The IF institutions operate cost efficiently, whereas conventional banking is more cost efficient in dual banking countries where there is no significant difference between business orientation and stability. On the other hand, Erol et al. (2014) hold that IF in Turkey performs better in profitability and asset management ratios compared to conventional counterparts.

Financial Sector and Islamic Finance in Turkey

A number of countries including some non-Muslim nations introduce regulations to make room for the IF within the financial system. Despite growing interest in its activities, however, the IF is subjected to a number of criticisms due to some of its practices and problems that need to be attended. The IF is particularly criticized because it prefers Mudaraba in collecting funds, whereas relies on Murabaha in distributing profits as a system based on the PLS model. This is generally referred to as a contradiction (Aras and Öztürk 2011). Experts and analysts indicate that the IF is unable to offer solutions where there are contradictions between the national legal systems and Islamic law, to introduce standardization in financial reporting, cannot properly implement the PLS model, lacks of high-quality staff and infrastructure and of financial engineering and product development process. But a sector like this one which grows exponentially will present solutions to its problems over the time.

The history of modern banking in Turkey can be traced back to the Ottoman era. The first bank was founded by the bankers in Galata in 1847. The bank, called Istanbul Bank, was liquidated in 1852. The modern banking activities were initiated in 1856 when Ottoman Bank was created (Yetiz 2016). Banking has become an important sector in the republican era where private banking was promoted. In general, the IF operates with the conventional banking at the same time. Turkey is one of the countries employing both CF and IF systems. The first interest-free banking institution was the State Industrial Workers Investment Bank that was established in 1975 to attract the savings and funds held by the individuals and small enterprises that avoided interest-based activities. The bank remained active up to 1978 (Polat 2009). Then, the first IF institutions were created in 1985 in the form of special financial institutions and were renamed under law number 5411 as participation banks. The IF institutions which remained private financial institutions until the legal amendment were renamed participation banks. With the completion of the legal infrastructure, the Turkish interest-free banking has become one of the most renowned models in the world in terms of banking methods and practices. As a result of this, the IF in Turkey has maintained profitability that is higher than the world average (Dünya İslami Bankacılık Rekabet Raporu 2015).

The IF institutions in Turkey rely on trade or partnership models to transfer the financial resources to the real sector. The trade activities generally involve individual financial support, corporate financial support and financial leasing. The IF institution purchases the goods, commodities, raw materials or services that the corporations and enterprises need on behalf of them and sells these to the same enterprises. The partnership model, on the other hand, is based on the PLS or risk capital (Yılmaz 2010). In addition, basic and conventional banking services including credit of letter or confidence letter are also provided by the IF institutions (Aras and Öztürk 2011). It provides financial support for the trade and the industrial factors under the legislations in lieu of loans. The risk that these funds may not be returned is low in real sector, which prevents waste of resources. The financing of the direct investments within real sector has positive impact on the macro indicators (Wouters 2007).

Frequent Sukuk exports made Turkey a lead actor in the global IF scheme. As a result of this, a number of institutions made investments in Turkey for the first time. With the help of growing interest, the share of the IF in Turkey's financial sector was 1.84 *pct* in 2001, whereas it has become 3.34 in 2007 and 5.2 in 2015. And as of December 2015, there were 52 active banks in Turkey (34 saving, 13 development and 5 participation banks) (Çelik 2016). Another important development in the sector in the country was the establishment of the World Bank's Global Islamic Finance Development Center under the auspices of the World Bank and Under secretariat of Treasury. The centre is expected to conduct training and research activities and offer counselling and technical assistance for the member countries in the World Bank Group. Overall, number of institutions focused on the needs of the sector increases and legal framework for the sector is maintained to ensure further interest. This naturally takes the popular attention to the IF.

Islamic Banking in Malaysia

In most parts of the world, financial markets are controlled by CF, whereas some developing nations like Malaysia employ a dual banking system because of the growing role of the IF as an alternative model. Considering the role of the CF in economic crises, there is growing interest in alternative systems like IF because of its social and moral elements and features. A review of the two sectors in dual banking systems reveals that the IF performs better than its counterpart in terms of profitability, risk management, asset growth and other elements. This better explains the popularity of the IF system in some countries (Hasan and Dridi 2010). The government also works to make sure that the Islamic banking is incorporated into mainstream banking (Dünya İslami Bankacılık Rekabet Raporu 2013).

The foundations of the IF system in Malaysia have been laid down through a set of initiatives including the establishment of Islamic Banking in 1983, Islamic Capital Market in 1993, Islamic Interbank Money Market in 1994, Kuala Lumpur Stock Exchange Rate Shariah Index in 1999 and finally the announcement of the financial sector master plan in 2001 by the Central Bank of Malaysia (Furqani and Mulyany 2009). The Muslim Pilgrims Saving Corporations, founded to meet the financial needs of the Muslim pilgrims in 1963, is the first interest-free financial institution in the country. In 1983, The Bank Islam Malaysia Berhad was established; the bank carried out interest-free activities for 10 years. Under the IF legislation, the Central Bank of Malaysia is authorized to apply the rules applicable to the CF banks to the IF institutions as well (Sobol 2014).

In 1993, the government introduced legislation required for the CF institutions to offer interest-free financial services; in 1999, the Ministry of Finance raised discussion on Interest-Free Banking Scheme. Under this legislation, the commercial banks, financial corporations and some banks were authorized to offer interest-free financial services. Subsequently, Bank Muamalat Malaysia Berhad, the second interest-free financial institution of the country, was established. In 1997, National Shariah Advisory Council (NSAC) was created to examine the compatibility of the interest-free banking transactions with the Islamic law (Mukhtar et al. 2006).

The successful policies led to positive results; in a number of IF practices, Malaysia has become one of the world leaders. Currently, the sector is still striving. In 2013, some legislations have been amended for clarification in the legal ground after which Muslim scholars can be now held accountable legally for the approved financial products. Some major changes are further expected in the individual portfolios after introduction of a bill that offers a distinction between savings and investments (Dünya İslami Bankacılık Rekabet Raporu 2015).

Like other developing nations, Malaysia also needs foreign capital for investments that would generate jobs. For this reason, a number of incentive programmes have been introduced to attract interest-free domestic and foreign funds. In the field of education, INCEIF, ISRA and IBFIM are established to offer quality training for the sector. These policies and incentives played a huge role in the development of IF. Currently, there are 21 IF institutions in the country, serving as providers of funds (Güngör 2015). These institutions offer Islamic alternatives to the financial products offered by CF institutions.

Islamic Finance Sector's Development in Indonesia

It could be argued that the Islamic countries have more options in terms of alternative financial capital sources because the IF has become a popular trend in the last few decades as evidenced by the amount of investments it has attracted in different parts of the world. Many countries in the world, including East Asian, have been making efforts for legal arrangements to promote the IF (Venardos 2012). Indonesia, the largest economy in South Asia, makes efforts to improve its own IF industry to catch up Malaysia which hosts the most developed Islamic banking market. The share of the IF within the financial system in Indonesia is 4.5 *pct*, however, it should be noted, this is insignificant given that Indonesia is a predominantly Muslim country.

According to data by Bank Indonesia, there are 11 IF institutions in the country in 2015, with 2139 branches; additionally, 23 CF institutions offer interest-free services through what is called Islamic window in 433 branches. Even though these figures indicate that the country has an advanced IF system, the reality is different. Indonesia ranks slightly ahead of Brunei and way behind Britain and Malaysia in terms of the popularity of the IF activities and services. According to Reni and Ahmad (2016), the reasons for the slow development of IF in Indonesia include religion, limited knowledge, attitude and weak government support.

The IF had encountered two main problems since the initial years: doubts that whether or not the financial products are in line with the Islamic rules, and their poor performance in banking activities when compared to their conventional counterparts. Because of the first problem, particularly religious people tend to stay away from their products. The IF institutions are unable to offer plausible solutions that would address these doubts. But its positive performance in the recent global crisis indicates that it has developed its competitiveness. Vizcaino and Suroyo (2014) states that lack of a strong support by government and public institutions is an important problem for the IF. For instance, the Indonesian government has postponed legal arrangements up to the 1990s for political reasons such as religious radicalism; because of this, the sector gained comparative advantage in Turkey and Malaysia. According to Rossi (2010), the dynamics directing the sector are inadequate and the regulations opening up the doors for the improvement of the IF are not sufficient. Another major obstacle before the development of the financial sector is population and geographical conditions. World Bank data shows that only 19.6 *pct* of the adult population is included in the financial system. More than 100 million people have no access to any sort of financial service. Due to geographical structure, most economic activities are centred around in a few major cities resulting in less frequent access to the financial services. For instance, 1700 rural banks constituting 93 *pct* of the total number of banks makes up only 1.5 *pct* of the total assets of the sector. It should also be noted that more than half of the total savings in the commercial banks is held in Jakarta.

In fact, the sector has a huge potential in case more people are involved through proper measures of financial integration. If the compliance with Islamic laws is clarified, particularly religious people will more likely pay greater attention. But some recent studies show that this optimistic expectation may be misleading. Lawrance (2014) upholds that large portion of the people consider religious sensitivity as a factor; but they, in the end, tend to act pragmatically. Thus, they may well prefer CF institutions over the IF if they conclude that it is a better idea because the CF also offer Islamic finance windows services.

The Indonesian Financial Service Authority introduced some new arrangements in order to support the IF development throughout the country in 2014. One of these policies focusing on the improvement of the capital structure of the IF institutions was particularly important.

According to this arrangement, the parts of the CF offering Islamic windows services should be separated from the original institution to be converted into an IF institution. The goal was to ensure that the IF would become more popular and more competitive. It is generally agreed that in case this policy succeeds, the IF will become even more popular.

Dual Banking System and Islamic Finance in Qatar

The dual banking system of Qatar appears to be one of the smallest among GCC[3] countries in terms of total assets, loans and deposits. But in sector terms, the system has grown stably as a result of the decisive implementation of the financial liberalization and deepening policies. The share of the private banks in the public tenders has declined. The sector has become more competitive because the banks now have to pay attention to individual banking instead of being involved in public projects.

The positive impact generated by the hydrocarbon industry upon all sectors made the greatest contribution to the development of the sector. For this reason, tracing the direction of the relationship between finance and growth is relatively easier in this case. The theoretical approach suggesting that the direction is from economic growth to the financial sector seems to be more explanatory. There are only a few studies on the IF–growth relationship in Qatar. Tabash and Dhankar (2014) hold a different view on the direction of the relationship. Their empirical findings show that the relationship is stable, indicating that it fits into the bidirectional approach.

Even though it is a small country, Qatar has 17 banks, six being run on local capital. Nine banks (three IF institutions) constitute 80 *pct* of the entire sector. Like other sectors that grow fast, the state, via large capital ventures, take the lead to make sure that the strongest financial institutions will become more active. In 1997, the state founded Qatar Industrial Development Bank to offer loans for small- and mid-sized enterprises. The Bank holds 50 *pct* of the deposits in the country. The Qatar Islamic Bank, founded with international capital partnership, currently controls 8.1 *pct* of the lending market and seeks to expand its activities to such countries as Turkey, Egypt and Kazakhstan. The Qatar Islamic Bank is the largest IF institution in the country.

Four IF banks and three CF banks operate on Islamic Windows; the priority in the sector is given to the real sector. A dramatic rise has been observed in the total assets of the IF in 2005 which is generally considered as a turning point (Tabash and Dhankar 2014). The share of the IF in the domestic financial sector has increased to 9 *pct* over the last years. In a comparative analysis, the sector has made rapid progress thanks to its capitalized, profitable and stable features (Iqbal 2001). The sector has become involved in underway projects including petrochemical, housing and construction projects (Tabash and Dhankar 2014). The IF, thus, appears to be a promising trend for the potential markets (Mohandas 2014).

The first and only stock exchange board was established in 1995 to contribute to economic development, to promote establishment of new companies and to offer transparent service for the investors. Two years later, it started its operations under the name of Doha Securities Market. Initially, only Qatar citizens were allowed to perform transactions at the market; but the citizens of Gulf states were further permitted to perform transactions, although they were subject to some restrictions. In 2002, the market introduced a fully electronic automation system. In June 2009, it was renamed to Qatar Exchange where NYSE Euronext holds 20 *pct* of the shares. In a very short time, the market has become one of the most dynamic exchange actors in the Middle East. But like many others, it was also affected by the crisis. Its performance declined by 34 *pct* in the insurance sector and 33 *pct* in industry. The total profitability of the companies quoted in the market declined by 8.9 *pct*. But the banks and financial institutions, supported by the government, were able to increase their profits by 4 *pct* (Aksoy 2011).

The Qatar Investment Authority, founded in 2005 to administer sovereign wealth funds, will expectedly increase its total assets beyond 8 trillion USD (Da 2011). Qatar Financial Center was established in 2005 to attract investments by international banks and large financial institutions so that they would contribute to major hydrocarbon projects and infrastructure investments. As part of this strategy, tax exemption was introduced and foreign investors were permitted to hold 100 *pct* of the property; additionally, low tax rates were set up for the profits. These incentives attracted the attention of major international investors. However, despite these measures, it was unable to compete with similar financial centres in Dubai and Bahrain.

Notes

1. On the other hand, some cooperative banking practices in some Muslim parts of India under the British rule are considered the first interest-free financing cases in the world.
2. IF intuitions increased liquidity holdings in the run-up to and during the crisis relative to conventional banks. This fact simply explains why did IF stocks performed better.
3. Gulf Cooperation Council countries are Bahrain, Kuwait, Oman, Qatar, Saudi Arabia and the United Arab Emirates.

References

Aksoy, M. 2011. MENA ülkelerinde Menkul Kıymet borsalar. In *Ortadoğu ve Kuzey Afrika Ülkelerinin Ekonomik Yapısı*, ed. H. Genç and F. Sayım. İstanbul: MKM Yayınları.

Aras, O.N., and M. Öztürk. 2011. Reel ekonomiye katkıları bakımından katılım banklarının kullandırdığı fonların analizi. *Ekonomi Bilimleri Dergisi* 3 (2): 166–179.

Askari, H., et al. 2012. *Risk sharing in finance: The Islamic finance alternative.* New York: Wiley.

Beck, T., A. Demirgüç-Kunt, and O. Merrouche. 2013. Islamic vs. conventional banking: Business model, efficiency and stability. *Journal of Banking & Finance* 37 (2): 433–447.

Bulut, H.İ., and B. Er. 2012. *Katılım Finansmanı: Katılım Bankacılığı ve Girişim Sermayesi* Türkiye Katılım Bankaları Birliği Yayın No: 3, ed. A. Yabanlı. İstanbul: Türkiye Katılım Bankaları Birliği.

Çelik, T. 2016. Türk bankacılık sektöründe etkinlik analizi: 2008–2014. *Uluslararası Alanya İşletme Fakültesi Dergisi* 8 (1): 1–12.

Da, H. 2011. Qatar as an oil emerging market. *International Journal of Marketing Studies* 3 (3): 141–151.

EY. 2015. *Dünya İslami Bankacılık Rekabet Raporu 2013–2014: Sektörel dönüşüm*, 5–17. İstanbul: Global İslamic Finance.

Ergeç, E.H., B.G. Kaytancı, and M. Toprak. 2014. Katılım Bankası müşterilerinin bankacılık sistemi kullanım tercihleri: Mevduat bankaları için İslami Bankacılık penceresi. *Tüketici ve Tüketim Araştırmaları Dergisi* 6 (2): 53–90.

Erol, C., et al. 2014. Performance comparison of Islamic (participation) banks and commercial banks in Turkish banking sector. *EuroMed Journal of Business* 9 (2): 114–128.

Faisal, Y.A. 2016. Islamic derivatives in Indonesia: A study on Indonesian Ulama Council (MUI)'s fatwa on tahawwut (hedging). *İslam Ekonomisi ve Finansı Dergisi* 2 (1): 35–61.

Furqani, H., and R. Mulyany. 2009. Islamic banking and economic growth: Empirical evidence from Malaysia. *Journal of Economic Cooperation and Development* 30 (2): 59–74.

Güngör, K. 2015. Malezya'daki Faizsiz bankacılık modelinin Türkiye'de uygulanabilirliği üzerine bir analiz. *Ayrıntı Dergisi* 29 (3): 54–61.

Hasan, M., and J. Dridi. 2010. The effects of the global crisis on Islamic and conventional banks: A comparative study. In *Monetary and capital markets department & Middle East and Central Asia department*, 1–47. Washington, DC: International Monetary Fund.

Iqbal, M. 2001. Islamic and conventional banking in nineties: A comparative study. *Islamic Economic Studies* 8 (2): 1–28.

Kasaroğlu, H. 2015. *İslami Finans: Kavram ve Temel İslami Finansman Araçları.*

Lawrance, J. 2014. Islamic finance in Indonesia: Past, present and future. In *Islamic Finance Indonesia*, 1–4. Kuala Lumpur: K§L Gates.

Mohandas, G. 2014. Role of finance in growth and development. In *Money, finance and economic growth: Emerging issues*, ed. Vidya Prasarak Mandal's K. G. Joshi College of Arts & N. G. Bedekar College of Commerce, India. 8–12.

Mukhtar, H.S.A., N. Abdullah, and S.M. Al-Habshi. 2006. Efficiency of Islamic banking in Malaysia: Stochastic frontier approach. *Journal of Economic Cooperation and Development* 27 (2): 37–70.

Nişancı, M., İ. Karabıyık, and M. Uçar. 2011. Finansal gelişme ve iktisadi büyüme: statik ve dinamik panel veri analizi. *SÜ İİBF Sosyal ve Ekonomik Araştırmalar Dergisi* 22 (1): 107–119.

Polat, A. 2009. Katılım Bankacılığı: Dünya Uygulamalarına Ilişkin Sorunlar-Fırsatlar; Türkiye Için Projeksiyonlar. In *Finansal Yenilik ve Açılımları ile Katılım Bankacılığı*, ed. A. Yabanlı, 12. İstanbul: Türkiye Katılım Bankaları Birliği.

Redford, E.S. 1966. Dual banking: A case study in federalism. *Law and Contemporary Problems* 31 (4): 749–773.

Reni, A., and H. Ahmad. 2016. Application of theory reasoned action in intention to use Islamic banking in Indonesia. *Al-Iqtishad: Journal of Islamic Economics* 8 (1): 137–148.

Rossi, V. 2010. *The challenges and opportunities for financial services in Indonesia.* London: Chatham House.

Sobol, I. 2014. Islamic banking: The case of Malaysia. In *Redefinition of the role of Asia-Pacific region in the global economy*, ed. B. Skulska, A.H. Jankowiak, and S. Mazurek, 243–244. Wrocław: Publishing House of Wrocław University of Economics.

Tabash, M.I., and R.S. Dhankar. 2014. Islamic banking and economic growth: An empirical evidence from Qatar. *Journal of Applied Economics and Business* 2 (1): 51–67.

Türker, H. 2010. *İslami Finans sisteminde finansal aracılık: dünyadaki gelişmeler ve sermaye piyasasının geliştirlmesi açısından Türkiye için öneriler*, 11–44. Ankara: Sermaye Piyasası Kurulu.

Venardos, A.M. 2012. *Islamic banking and finance in South-East Asia: Its development & future*, 3rd ed. Asia-Pacific Business Series. London: World Scientific.

Vizcaino, B., and G. Suroyo. 2014. Indonesia revises Islamic banking rules as industry growth slides. In *Financials*. Jakarta: Thomson Reuters.

Wouters, P. 2007. Katılım Bankacılığı Gerçek Bir İhtiyaç. In *Dünyada ve Türkiye'de Faizsiz Bankacılık*, 11–30. İstanbul: Türkiye Katılım Bankalar Birliği.

Yetiz, F. 2016. Bankacılığın doğuşu ve Türk bankacılık sistemi. *Niğde Üniversitesi İktisadi ve İdari Bilimler Fakültesi Dergisi* 9 (2): 107–120.

Yılmaz, O.N. 2010. *Faizsiz Bankacılık İlkeleri ve Katılım Bankacılığı*. Antalya: Türkiye Katılım Bankalar Birliği.

Authors' Biography

Dr. Halil Şimşek holds a BA in Islamic Studies from Al-Azhar University of Cairo and another BA in political studies from City University of New York. He continued his graduate studies at the Department of Near and Middle Eastern Civilizations of the University of Toronto. His PhD research focused on the exegetical studies and Quranic commentaries of the Ottoman period, and in particular the Quranic commentary of Abu-Suud Efendi, the most celebrated and the highest religious authority during the reign of Sulaiman the Magnificent of the 16th century CE. His other research interests involve Islam and modernity, Muslim political thought, Islamic literature, and hermeneutics.

Dr. Servet Bayındır is Professor of Islamic Law., He completed his double majored undergraduate studies (Islamic Studies and Economics) at Marmara University and Anadolu University. He earned PhD degree at Marmara, and did postdoctoral studies on Islamic Finance in International Islamic Finance Education Centre (INCEIF) in Malaysia. His researches manly focuses on Islamic Finance, and to name a few of his published books: "Futures Contracts from the viewpoint of Islamic Law: Forward, Future, Option and Swap" (Istanbul, 2008), "Commerce in Islam with regards to Fiqh and Morality" (Istanbul, 2007), "Interest Free Banking in terms of Islamic Law" (Istanbul, 2005).

Dr. Murat Ustaoğlu is an Associate Professor of Islamic Economics. He was born in Turkey, and educated at the Ramapo College of New Jersey (B.A.) and the City University of New York (M.A.), and holds a Ph.D. degree in Economics. Dr. Ustaoğlu has worked at Bank of New York and JP Morgan Chase Bank in US. He is, most recently, co-author of Islamic Finance Alternatives for Emerging Economies (2014), Post-Conflict Syrian State and Nation Building (2015) and many research articles focusing Islamic Finance and Economics. Additionally, he teaches undergraduate and graduate level various courses in Economics.

CHAPTER 3

Financing Economic Growth in Emerging Economies: A Theoretical Approach

Selim Demez, Hülya Deniz Karakoyun and Elif Haykır Hobikoğlu

Abstract As a result of differentiation in the financial sector in some parts of the world, particularly the Muslim world with the rise of IF in the 1970s, a two-dimensional financial system known as dual banking emerged. The conventional financial (CF) system constituted the vast majority of the financial sector in the whole world; however, IF has grown dramatically in the last decades, becoming an alternative financing model. Despite the differences between the two models, the main goal in both systems is to serve as mediators for fund suppliers and fund receivers. CF is an interest-based system and is able to fund all sectors of the economy, while IF institutions, on the other hand, have to comply with secular and Islamic legal rules.

Keywords Islamic finance · Financial development · Economic growth

S. Demez (✉) · H.D. Karakoyun · E.H. Hobikoğlu
Istanbul University, Istanbul, Turkey
e-mail: selimdemez@windowslive.com

M. Ustaoğlu and A. İncekara (eds.), *Balancing Islamic and Conventional Banking for Economic Growth*, DOI 10.1007/978-3-319-59554-2_3

Introduction

Sustainable economic growth is important for developing countries in their path to becoming advanced and developed economies. The main advantages of sustainable growth include increased consumption, production, higher rates of employment, greater amounts of capital accumulation, more funds for social projects and the promotion of innovations that make life easier and more comfortable (Aslan and Yilmaz 2015). Stable growth depends on the success and harmony of all economic actors in the country. Sometimes, setback in one sector may lead to setbacks in other sectors in a chain reaction. The problems in some sectors may have limited impact, whereas problems in financial sector may closely affect all other sectors, as evidenced in the 2008 crisis. For this reason, a healthy financial sector is crucially important for the entire national economy. For this reason, financial sector attracts close attention in the growth literature. It helps accumulation of capital for development and spread of technology. In theory, advanced financial systems allow the individuals to diversify investments. In this way, the investment risks for the holders of deposits decline and make positive contribution to growth.

Linkage between financial development and growth has been a discussion in the literature where three main views on the direction of this linkage are under review. The first approach defended by Schumpeter (1912) is based on a pretty simple assumption. According to this hypothesis, known as the supply-leading approach, the direction of the financial development-growth linkage moves towards from financial development to growth. Additionally, the dynamics out of the financial development create positive impacts upon growth. On the other hand, Robinson (1982) offers 'demand-following' approach which defends just the opposite. As the gist of the hypothesis (where real sector leads, finance follows) suggests, the direction of the linkage is the opposition; in other words, financial development is fostered by growth. Therefore, financial development has no impact on growth. Finally, according to the bidirectional relationship approach, there is a dual linkage. Growth affects financial development and financial development influences growth. Under this theory, both may affect each other most of the time.

This part of the study is focused on the contribution by the financial institutions to the growth by sectors in Turkey, Malaysia, Indonesia and Qatar, leading to the theoretical foundation of the empirical model. In subsequent sections, the linkage between financial development and growth in similar time intervals composed of the same dataset for every country is measured with the comparative empirical analyses for the impact of the IF and the CF sector. Proper interpretation of the findings depends upon the solid theoretical foundations. For this reason, a literature review for linkage between financial development and growth after a narration of the main concepts. Finally, the linkage between financial development and growth in emerging economies is analysed to offer theoretical foundations covering the economic policies of the empirical analyses in the subsequent sections.

Financial System and Economy

In modern societies, the specialization of the labour is distinguished from investment and saving processes. And the linkage between suppliers of funds and fund receivers takes place in the financial system. Financial system as a key for the distribution of the financial resources represents the institutions and markets regulating the fund currents and movements, the tools facilitating these movements and the legal and administrative rules that apply to those. The development of financial markets contributes to the acceleration of the technological advance by ensuring effective distribution of resources in terms of place and time. Because of this function, the relationship between financial development and growth is analysed in empirical and theoretical studies.

Financial development which allows diversification of the tools used in the financial markets and their frequent use can be described as the development and growth of the financial institutions, markets, services and tools. Some economists offer a different description that refers to the effectiveness of the financial system or the advances in the field as well (Khan 2000). Financial deepening is a term that is different from financial development. Financial deepening can be defined as the ratio of transferring the funds generated in the financial sector to the real sector. In other words, it is an increase in the ratio of the financial services and institutions per head or financial assets to the income (Ahmed and Ansari 1998). Financial deepening allows easy access to services provided by financial markets and mediators. The efficiency of financial system is measured in their influence in decreasing the information and transaction costs for their customers.

In modern-time liberal economies, financial development and deepening play an important role in the stability of growth rates. The terms explained so far are used by both CF and IF. It is also useful to talk about some IF terms as well because of the differences between the two models.

Because IF has to provide funds based on PLS model, their funds are generally used in projects and real development mechanisms. For this reason, they do not respond to demands for funds other than real investment tools because of their legal status. Savings make positive contributions to national economy on a macro level by supporting the real economy. In essence, the PLS model is based on sharing risk and revenue and thus can be defined as a financing method where the financial intermediates join as partners. In the project that is financed, financial capital is supplied by the bank, whereas the customer contributes their labour and expertise. In the model, the projects picked by the bank are supported based on profit- and loss-sharing principle. But the mission of the bank is not limited to providing finance. To see whether or not the project moves forward in line with the project, a monitoring group is set up to follow up the investments.

The main tools of the IF intermediate financing models include partnership model, commercial model, sharing model and sharing risk and uncertainty in stock exchange. In short, Mudaraba is monetization of the partnership of labour and capital, Muzara'ah of the agricultural partnership, Mushakat of the irrigation partnership, Maharasa of the plantation partnership, Ijara of financial leasing, Murabaha of production support and Tawarruq of the goods. As seen above, the IF can only support real sector investments; because of this feature, it can be argued that this makes greater contribution to the growth.

In both financial models, there are theoretical and empirical findings pointing out to a positive relationship between financial development and growth; these findings offer some insights on the future of technological change as well as financial development level, growth and capital movements. As the level of financial development improves, these indicators generally become even more positive. On the other hand, it is still controversial as to whether or not growth leads to financial development or financial development to growth. There are accounts in the literature that support both approaches. These approaches present different views on the direction of the linkage between growth and financial development. Before moving to finance-growth theory, it is useful to look at the literature first.

Literature for Finance and Economic Growth Relations: Conventional Finance

Anything in economics that is not sustainable cannot be regarded as successful. This notion applies to growth as well. Sustainable growth is something new for the history of the world. Even though it is fairly important for social development, its improvement has been considerably slow up to the nineteenth century. In 1800s, it was introduced in a few countries including UK and France; but sustainable development did not attract any significant attention in other parts of the world (Ahmed and Ansari 1998). Aghion et al. (2009) maintain that when per capita income is compared by different time intervals, there is almost no increase in the first thousand years, whereas 50*pct* of increase has been observed in the second millennium. Average annual growth rate increased by 0.5*pct* in the period between 1820 and 1870; this was 3*pct* annually in the period between the Second World War and the present. There is general agreement that the current growth rates improved the level of welfare; there are different theses on the direction of the relationship between finance and growth. Levine (2005) offers two reasons for this. First, there are works suggesting that the physical capital accumulation in large amounts will not make positive contribution to growth in the long term. There is no work noting that in the finance-growth linkage, financial development influences decisions on distribution of sources, aggregate savings and productivity. Secondly, there are two factors weakening the view that growth and emergence of financial arrangements improve resource allocation and minimize the risk. Higher returns fail to provide the expected impact in saving rates due to income and substitutions effects; and the lower risk factor also falls short on increasing saving rates. For this reason, there are different views on the direction of the relationship.

The literature started to focus on the relationship between financial development and growth in the late nineteenth century. First theoretical accounts argued that financial development would have positive impact on growth in the long term (Tsuru 2000). There are four different views that emerged historically on this matter in the literature. First, is the supply-leading hypothesis indicating that financial development contributes to growth and that there is causality in that direction (Musalima et al. 2014). It was offered by Goldsmith, McKinon-Shaw and Fry and argues that financial markets play a positive role in growth. However, the foundation of the theory can also be traced back to Bagehot (1873) and Schumpeter (1912; Evans et al. 2002). According to this hypothesis, financial development contributes positively to growth. It further argues that there is direct causality from financial development towards growth and that this causality increases investments and promotes capital accumulation (Shaw 1973).

One of the views that attract attention in the literature is the argument offered by King and Levine (1993) that financial intermediates affect growth positively through capital accumulation. Financial intermediates contribute to growth by increasing the effectiveness of capital accumulation and the saving and investment ratios. There are empirical works supporting this argument. Bagehot and Hicks argue that capital movement plays a critical role in industrialization in Britain and pays attention to the role of the banking system in growth. Banks fund efficient investments and contribute to innovation and future growth. According to Schumpeter (1912), banks act as financial intermediates to facilitate technological innovation. Because banks are careful in selecting firms that will use social savings, they make positive contribution to growth by ensuring effective distribution of the savings. In this way, banks make a positive contribution through increased efficiency and technological changes.

The second approach is the demand-following hypothesis offered by Robinson (1952) which argues that financial development follows growth. This view suggests that financial development is just a side show; and we can speak of a direct linkage between growth towards financial development. The hypothesis is briefly articulated as where enterprise leads, finance follows and basically says that finance is not the driving force behind growth but growth creates demand for financial sector. Goldsmith (1969), McKinnon (1973) and Shaw (1973) have made contributions to the hypothesis. Particularly McKinnon (1973) and Shaw (1973) apply the hypothesis to the developing countries. Like the theoretical works, empirical works have also employed different econometric methods; for this reason, there is no commonly agreed approach on the presence and direction of the linkage and causality. As noted before, the direction and the strength of the causality between financial development and growth remains extremely controversial.

According to Demetrades and Hussein (1996), both views are applicable; they simply refer to a mutual causality known as a bidirectional relationship. The causality between financial development and growth can be bidirectional; in other words, financial development may foster growth and growth may also positively contribute to financial development. On the other hand, Lucas (1988) is of the view that there is no causality between financial development and growth and holds that the economists should pay greater attention to the roles of the financial mediators in the growth.

The conflicting views in the supply-leading and demand-leading arguments can be settled by the development phase hypothesis. This argument suggests that in the early stages of growth, financial development leads to real capital accumulation. According to the hypothesis, innovations and new financial services provide new opportunities for investors and saving holders, creating self-sustaining growth. As financial and economic development progresses, the demand-oriented side becomes more dominant (Calderon and Liu 2003).

The new growth theories, on the other hand, argue that financial mediation and financial markets respond to the problems in the economy and positively affect growth. The financial institutions and markets that emerge to deal with the problems caused by transactional costs use potential entrepreneurs to ensure effective investment decisions. By relying on similar theoretical models, Greenwood and Jovanovic (1990), Shaw (1973), Levine (1991, 1997), Bencivenga and Smith (1991) and Saintpaul (1992) agree that the effective work of the financial markets positively affect growth through improvement in the quality of investments. Growth promotes investments, whereas the increased investments also contribute to growth.

Financial intermediates offer their expertise and knowledge to the investors so that they could use effectively. The investors make profit thanks to the financial intermediates. The profit and revenue made out of the capital investments increase level of income and growth. Levine (2005) offers five main categories for the functions of the markets. Financial markets contribute to source distribution by facilitating trade and offering protection against risks. Financial executives establish a control mechanism over financial activities and ensure the movement of the savings by facilitating the exchange of goods and services. While some fundamental functions do not differ by country and time, financial institutions governed by markets that perform these functions present different features in different countries and times.

Financial development governed by the financial system refers to capital accumulation and technological advance as a means of affecting growth. The financial system, by changing the saving ratio or redefining saving in the different capital production technologies, changes the capital accumulation. Technological advance pays attention to new products and production processes and the functions performed by the financial system affect the stable growth by affecting the rate of technological innovation. Technological progress ensures the diversification of financial tools which create an area that is influential to growth by ensuring the spread of the financial system and the financial deepening.

Greenwood and Jovanovic (1990) note that growth provides a fertile ground for financial structure and that advanced financial systems accelerate growth. Blackburn and Hung (1998) and Harrison et al. (1999) uphold that the financial intermediates reduce the evaluation costs of the projects and therefore contribute to growth. In a growing economy, the number of investment projects affects the intensity and profitability of the financial intermediary's services.

Therefore, the literature on the linkage between finance and growth improves. The theoretical and empirical approaches in the literature are based on the CF system. Number of works on the linkage between IF and growth is relatively small. Empirical works, on the other hand, are focused on the Islamic countries. It is therefore useful to look at the literature focusing on the linkage between IF and growth for a comparative analysis and better results.

Islamic Finance and Economic Growth

Efforts are made to make sure that the collected funds are used in investments with high returns. According to the PLS model, the profit made out of capital involvement and the expertise of the capital holder is shared. The system which works in reference to partnership instead of interest eliminates the investment options outside of the real economy and minimizes the speculative risk ratios. Some of the factors in the conventional methods that negatively affect financial development and growth include risk, uncertainty, government interference and inability of funding efficient entrepreneurial activities. Due to its structural features, the IF is distinguished from conventional counterparts. Because they closely follow the productivity of the enterprises they fund, they reduce the risks and elements of uncertainty.

The majority of the studies focusing on the relationship between financial development and growth assume that the CF may play significant roles in growth. On the other hand, IF also makes positive contributions to growth by using the elements that minimize the risk. The IF's finance model is based on the stronger bond between finance and real economy. The CF and growth relationship is covered extensively in the literature; but number of works analyzing IF's relationship with growth is pretty small because its share within the financial sector is relatively insignificant. The literature is generally focused on the developing Islamic economies to determine the direction of the relationship and to measure the impact on growth. The first major work on this is the one by Furqani and Mulyany (2009) which analyses the policies to promote IF in Malaysia. The study determines a positive and significant relationship between IF and growth and capital accumulation and further notes that policies for greater involvement of IF in international trade should be devised.

On the other hand, Majid and Kassim (2010), also focusing on Malaysia by relying on the same time interval and dataset, are of a different view on the direction of the relationship. Furqani and Mulyany (2009) argue that the direction is demand-following, whereas Majid and Kassim (2010) support the supply-leading argument (Manap et al. 2012). Farahani and Sadr (2012) acquired similar findings in an empirical study focusing on Indonesia and Iran, also noting that the IF contributes positively to economic development in the short term. In the long term, on the other hand, there is positive relationship between growth and capital accumulation. In addition, they recommend the Indonesian government to follow Malaysia's policies to increase the share of the IF within the financial sector.

In their empirical work, Abduh and Omar (2012) offer an alternative approach contradicting Schumpeter's supply-leading and Robinson's demand-following approaches that determines a bidirectional relationship between the development of IF and growth in both short and long terms. This means that they argue there is a bidirectional relationship where IF development supports growth while growth leads to growth in Indonesia. Likewise, Abduh and Chowdhury (2012) identifies a bidirectional linkage for the Bangladeshi economy.

Zizek et al. (2016), in their work consisting of an analysis of 17 members in the Organization of Islamic Cooperation for the period between 1999 and 2011 by reliance on panel data, refer to a strong relationship between IF and growth. They argue that it supports population growth and capital stock which further contribute to growth. As growth increases, unemployment rate declines. In the short term, there is negative relationship between government expenditure and growth. According to the findings of the study, government expenditure is negatively affected, whereas private sector expenditures are positively influenced. Finally, Caporale and Helmi (2016) analyse the relationship between real credit to the private sector and real GDP in order to test the impact of IF institutions upon growth in emerging economies. The findings confirm that there is a strong relationship between real credit to real GDP in the long term and a weaker relationship between IF and emerging economies in the short term.

The common argument in the empirical works on the emerging economies suggests that there is a strong and positive relationship between IF and growth in the long term. This is not the case with the short term. It is also not possible to speak of a common argument even in the works conducted by use of the similar datasets for the similar periods in different countries with respect to the direction of the relationship. Some studies support Schumpeter's supply-leading approach, whereas some others present more realistic results for Robinson's demand-following approach. Others, on the other hand, refer to a bidirectional relationship as a third option.

Finance and Economic Growth Relation in Theory

The significance of the financial markets can be better acknowledged at the stage of determining efficiency through endogenous growth model. The model can be utilized to better understand the financial development generated by CF sector upon growth (Tsuru 2000). Pagano (1993) who evaluates the financial growth relations analyses the impacts of the financial development upon growth via this model. The model is based upon evaluation of the production and investment relationship through such variables as growth rate (g), productivity of capital (A), portion of savings (φ), saving rate (s), depreciation rate (δ).

$$g = A\phi s - \delta \tag{3.1}$$

where

- g Growth rate,
- A Productivity of capital,
- ϕ Portion of savings,
- s Saving rate,
- δ Depreciation rate

The model simply explains the impact on growth when part of the savings is directed at the investments (Tsuru 2000). According to the model, the financial development is affected by the change in each of the variables in each side of the equation. In this model, the total production (Y_t) is a linear function of the capital stock (K_t) and its equation is expressed as ($Yt = AtKt$).

The model shows that the developments in financial sector may affect growth in two ways. First, the banking sector in a competitive market will play influential role in channelling savings to investments; this will increase ϕ. As Eq. (3.1) shows, as ϕ increases, growth rate (g) will also increase. Secondly, the financial institutions move the funds to the investments with highest marginal efficiency of the capitals (A) and increases growth. Efficient source transfer increases the strength of the financial system. Savings can be distributed more effectively and more accurately through the financial institutions. And the increased capital efficiency positively affects growth. A financial system that improves via the diversity of financial means increases the saving rates and methods; this influences the social marginal efficiency of investments and increases the growth positively.

Financial system in Islamic countries is composed of a dual institutional structure, which is where the loaning and borrowing transactions are performed differently. The main difference is observed in the way the funds collected by the financial institutions are used. CF finance can provide loans for all sectors, whereas the IF can only fund products and sectors justified by borders of Islamic law. Likewise, according to the Islamic law, savings can only be used in transactions and activities that are considered part of commercial engagements.

Economic Growth and Finance Nexus in Emerging Economies

Financial deepening is achieved as the financial markets are able to transfer the saving resources to the efficient areas. Developing nations need external and internal financial capital to fund development and growth. It is possible to speak of an advanced and sophisticated financial sector in the developed nations; but this is not the case with most of the developing nations. Developing countries adopt policies supportive of financial liberalization that mandates restructuring in the sector to better use foreign funds. They often pursue competitive monetary policies because of the economic attraction of the developed countries. When these policies become unsustainable, a strong financial crises may break out in different parts of the world as evidenced in 1990s and 2000s in Mexico and Far East.

A significant portion of the works focusing on the relationship between developments in financial sector and growth pay attention to the relationship between banking system and growth. The banks provoke domestic savings through their policies and thus contribute to sustainable growth by attracting foreign funds and capital. According to the development economy literature, one of the most important dynamics of growth is capital accumulation (Beck et al. 2000). Lack of sufficient amount of capital to finance development particularly in the developing nations is the greatest obstacle before sustainable development and growth policies of the government. To overcome this problem, it is important to offer financial resources to the service of efficient sectors that support growth. When conducting the financial mediation services, the banks try to transfer the capital to efficient areas. The financial sector deals with the problems caused by the weaknesses in the institutional structure in the developing countries. The sector also ensures effective transformation of the capital and increases the investments.

Capital accumulation is considered one of the preconditions for growth; the low level of efficiency in the financial system in developing countries is taken as one of the obstacles to the capital accumulation. These countries are categorized as financially repressed economies. In these economies, government interventions to control interest rates and the loan distributions lead to the shrinking of the markets and harm the activities of financial mediation.

McKinnon (1973) and Shaw (1973) suggest that for a balanced interest rate, interventions in the markets should be removed and the loans should be distributed by consideration of effectiveness. According to this hypothesis that applied to developing nations like Turkey in the 1970s and 1980s, financial development makes positive contribution to growth. On the other hand, they further argue that for the developing countries where financial development and deepening is achieved via financial deregulation, proper models applicable to the unique conditions of those countries should be developed. The financial liberalization debates that intensified in the 1970s in the world led to the adoption of deregulation policies in a number of developing nations in the 1980s. The liberalization of interest rates, the convertibility of the domestic currency and the liberalization of capital movements are the most popular practices and policies.

The theoretical foundations of financial liberalization were laid down by McKinnon and Shaw who offered a different theory for the developing nations in the 1970s by objecting to the neoclassical/Keynesian approaches. The main point of reference of the theory is financial repression in the developing countries (Fry 1982). According to McKinnon (1973), financial sector did not adequately flourish in economies suffering from financial repression. For this reason, financial institutions in the economy are unable to perform the functions they are expected to play. As a result, the economy is badly affected by this. The real sector face difficulties in fulfilling the financial needs.

The most important player of the financial markets is banks. When the real interest rates are low in the financial markets, restrictions over the interest rates, as well as the chronic inflation rate, reduce the interest in the financial assets (McKinnon 1989). Due to financial repression, interest rates are not determined by supply and demand in the market. Low real interest rates and lack of financial deepening make the idle means including gold, currency and real estate more attractive than financial instruments. Due to lack of funds that can be loaned, credit rationing occurs (Uygur 1993). In a country suffering from this type of financial pressure, the interest rate of the monetary assets is generally negative. The unwillingness of the people to open a saving account or make investment in the stock exchange makes the realization of financial deepening less likely. For this reason, in developing countries, the impact of the financial repression upon real capital accumulation is negative (Collier and Mayer 1989). McKinnon (1989) argues that the financial repression leads to the following results:

i. Capital market does not improve and financial deepening is ensured via the banking sector that provides funds for short-term needs due to lack of liquidity and high inflation rate.
ii. Because loaning market is not advanced, the entrepreneurs are unable to secure financial support.
iii. Due to these restrictions in the loaning market, the creditors prefer rationing.
iv. Negative interest rates increase the amount of savings of the households and entrepreneurs, preventing the accumulation of liquid assets necessary for investments.

Because there is no financial deepening in the economies suffering from financial pressure, the banking deposits remain crucial for savings. When monetary savings ensuring high level of income for the saving deposits become more attractive, the capital accumulation needed to fulfill investment projects including the modern technologies leads to increased and improved investment efficiency and productivity (Fry 1992).

In economies with a weak capital market, banking sector play a mediation role. Likewise, there is a relationship of complementarity between financial and economic capital. And this relationship makes the investments a possibility only in case of high returns. Positive real interest prepares ground for economic development by ensuring the transformation of the monetary accumulation into capital accumulation. McKinnon and Shaw, drawing attention to financial liberalization, note that the financial pressure will hurt economic balances. For this reason, they are opposed to any intervention into the financial markets including reserve requirements that banks have to observe. The hypothesis suggests that the relationship between real interest rates and saving rates increases the likelihood for the savings. Increase in the amount of savings further increases the amount of fund needed for investments and also strengthens the banking sector that serve as mediator in the allocation of funds to the firms. Financial liberalization increases the rate of saving in the economy and promotes investments. According to the hypothesis, the function of the banks can be summarized as follows:

i. There is a positive relationship between saving and real profit rate in the economy.
ii. Increased real revenue rate leads to greater amount of savings and combines the idle savings in the banking sector.
iii. Assuming that the financial markets work efficiently, amount of funds that can be transferred to the profitable areas increases.
iv. Increased amount of usable fund contributes to the growth by increasing amount of investment.

McKinnon (1989) notes that the neoclassical assumptions on monetary theory in respect to the developing countries are not valid and that money plays a different role in the process of capital accumulation in these economies. In these countries, the initial phases of the capital accumulation are composed of financial accumulation. Lack of a distinction between saving holders and the investors, lack of external sources and indivisibility of physical investments are some of the flaws in these countries. In economic and financial systems suffering from these problems, saving holders prefer monetary tools up to the point where they will be able to make investments upon more attractive economic tools.

In such economies where capital markets did not improve sufficiently, banks become dominant players; bank deposits remain the main and chief financial and monetary means of saving. Financial prosperity is a precondition for physical investment in the developing economies. And the precondition to financial welfare is the removal of all official and non-official restrictions and implementation of all financial reforms that will ensure financial liberalization. Only when this is done a balanced interest rate reflecting the true cost of capital can be attained.

McKinnon upholds that in the financial reform process, the budget deficit has to be addressed before liberalization of foreign trade (Uygur 1993). The economic structures of the developing countries are different from the economic structures of the developed countries. Particularly financial markets can be extremely weak in these countries. For this reason, the theoretical basis of the analyses relies on the assumption that the capital markets of these countries are fragmented. To increase the currency reserves, exports are promoted; as a result, the resources of the financial sector are channelled to this. The firms in other sectors have to receive loans on high interest rates. Lack of capital accumulation in the developing countries therefore leads to an unhealthy market structure (Clarke 1996).

Molho (1986), on the other hand, suggests that there are some differences in terms of the relationship between monetary and capital accumulation. Unlike McKinnon, Shaw argues that there is no relationship of complementarity between financial and physical capital. Deposits are the most important sources of fund for the financial intermediates. Increase in deposits will become an incentive for the investment because it will offer sources for the productive sectors. McKinnon is focused on the relationship between interest rates and investments financed by auto-financing sources, whereas Shaw attracts attention to the importance of relationship between external fiscal sources and financial deepening. Despite some differences, both views eventually complement each other. In the end, both scholars uphold that positive financial liberalization policies should be taken into consideration for a sound growth in the developing countries. The hypothesis offered by McKinnon and Shaw on financial liberalization and growth is an important one for the reform policies offered for the least developed countries by the IMF and World Bank since the 1980s (Wijenbergen 1991). In short, McKinnon and Shaw offer a fairly new approach by rejecting the neoclassical and Keynesian approaches that have been endorsed for both developed and developing countries up to the 1970s (Abedifar et al. 2015).

In conclusion, financial sources and investments are crucially important for sustainable growth. Financial sector is positively influenced by the process of globalization. The advances in the field of technology and information remove the physical barriers and borders by ensuring mobility of financial resources. For sustainable growth, both developed and developing nations will need external financial capital. For this reason, a number of countries seek to implement economic policies to better use global capital. To compete with the sophisticated financial sector in the developed countries, the developing countries implement financial policies that offer profitable products and services. This sometimes causes economic crises. It can be argued that compared to the conventional counterparts, the IF offers better advantages in terms of eliminating the risk for a crisis. For this reason, adoption of policies that will help the development of IF institutions will contribute to growth and to the social prosperity.

References

Abduh, M., and N.T. Chowdhury. 2012. Islamic banking—Economic growth nexus: Evidence from Bangladesh. *Journal of Islamic Economics, Banking and Finance* 8 (3): 104–113.

Abduh, M., and M.A. Omar. 2012. Islamic banking and economic growth: The Indonesian experience. *International Journal of Islamic and Middle Eastern Finance and Management* 5 (1): 35–47.

Abedifar, P., et al. 2015. Islamic banking and finance: Recent empirical literature and directions for future research. *Journal of Economic Surveys* 29 (4): 637–670.

Aghion, P., P. Howitt, and L. Bursztyn. 2009. *The economics of growth*, xxii, 495. Cambridge, MA: MIT Press.

Ahmed, S.M., and M.I. Ansari. 1998. Financial sector development and economic growth: The South-Asian experience. *Journal of Asian Economics* 9 (3): 503–517.

Aslan, N., and O. Yilmaz. 2015. Finansal gelişme ve büyüme ilişkisinin Solow modeli ile analizi: Türkiye üzerine bir çalışma. *Finansal Araştırmalar ve Çalışmalar Dergisi* 7 (12): 17.

Bagehot, W. 1873. *Lombart street: A description of the money market*. New York: E. P. Dutton.

Beck, T., R. Levine, and N. Loayza. 2000. Finance and the sources of growth. *Journal of Financial Economics* 58 (1–2): 261–300.

Bencivenga, V., and B. Smith. 1991. Financial intermediation and endogenous growth. *Review of Economic Studies* 58 (2): 195–209.

Blackburn, K., and V.T.Y. Hung. 1998. A theory of growth, financial development and trade. *Economica* 65 (257): 107–124.

Calderon, C., and L. Liu. 2003. The direction of causality between financial development and economic growth. *Journal of Development Economics* 72 (1): 321–334.

Caporale, G.M., and M.H. Helmi. 2016. *Islamic banking, credit and economic growth: Some empirical evidence*. Berlin: DIW German Institute for Economic Research.

Clarke, R. 1996. Equilibrium interest rates and financial liberalisation in developing countries. *Journal of Development Studies* 32 (3): 391–413.

Collier, P., and C. Mayer. 1989. The assessment: Financial liberalization, financial systems and economic growth. *Oxford Review of Economic Policy* 5 (4): 1–12.

Demetriades, P., and K. Hussein. 1996. Does financial development cause economic growth? Time series evidence from 16 countries. *Journal of Development Economics* 51: 387–411.

Evans, A.D., C.J. Green, and V. Murinde. 2002. Human capital and financial development in economic growth: New evidence using the translog production function. *International Journal of Finance & Economics* 7 (2): 123–140.

Farahani, G.Y., and S.M.H. Sadr. 2012. Analysis of Islamic bank's financing and economic growth: Case study Iran and Indonesia. *Journal of Economic Cooperation and Development* 33 (4): 1–24.

Fry, M.J. 1982. Models of financially repressed developing-economies. *World Development* 10 (9): 731–750.

Fry, M.J. 1992. The right interest rate policy for rapid economic growth. In *International finance group working paper*, 3. Birmingham: The University of Birmingham.

Furqani, H., and R. Mulyany. 2009. Islamic banking and economic growth: Empirical evidence from Malaysia. *Journal of Economic Cooperation and Development* 30 (2): 59–74.

Goldsmith, R.W. 1969. *Financial structure and development.* Studies in comparative economics, xxxiii, 561. New Haven: Yale University Press.

Greenwood, J., and B. Jovanovic. 1990. Financial development, growth and the distribution of income. *Journal of Political Economy* 98: 1067–1107.

Harrison, P., O. Sussman, and J. Zeira. 1999. Finance and growth: Theory and new evidence. In *Finance and economics discussion series.* Chicago, IL: Board of Governors of the Federal Reserve System.

Khan, A. 2000. The finance and growth Nexus. In *Business review*, 3–14. Philadelhia: Federal Reserve Bank of Philadelphia.

King, R.G., and R. Levine. 1993. Finance and growth: Schumpeter might be right. *The Quarterly Journal of Economics* 108 (3): 717–737.

Levine, R. 1991. Stock markets, growth, and tax policy. *Journal of Finance* 46 (4): 1445–1465.

Levine, R. 1997. Financial development and economic growth: Views and agenda. *Journal of Economic Literature* 35 (2): 688–726.

Levine, R. 2005. *Chapter 12 finance and growth: Theory and evidence*, vol. 1, 865–934.

Lucas, R.E. 1988. On the mechanics of economic development. *Journal of Monetary Economics* 22: 3–42.

Majid, S.A., and S. Kassim. 2010. Islamic finance and economic growth: The Malaysian experience. In *Kuala Lumpur Islamic Finance Forum.* Kuala Lumpur.

Manap, T.A.A., M. Abduh, and M.A. Omar. 2012. Islamic banking-growth nexus: Evidence from Toda—Yamamoto and bootstrap Granger causality test. *Journal of Islamic Finance* 1 (1): 59–66.

McKinnon, R.I. 1973. *Money and capital in economic development*, xii, 184. Washington: Brookings Institution.

McKinnon, I.R. 1989. Financial liberalization and economic development: A reassessment of interest rate policies in Asia and Latin America. *OREP* 5 (4): 29–54.

Molho, L.E. 1986. Interest rates, saving and investment in developing countries: A reexamination of the McKinnon-Shaw hypotheses. In *IMF staff papers,* 98. Washington, DC: IMF.
Musalima, R.A., E.M. Nyamongo, and E.D. Moyi. 2014. The relationship between financial development and economic growth in Africa. *Research in Applied Economics* 6 (2): 190–208.
Pagano, M. 1993. Financial-markets and growth—An overview. *European Economic Review* 37 (2–3): 613–622.
Robinson, J. 1952. *The rate of interest, and other essays.* London: MacMillan.
Robinson, J. 1982. *The rate of interest and other essays,* viii, 170. Westport, CT: Hyperion Press.
Saintpaul, G. 1992. Technological choice, financial-markets and economic-development. *European Economic Review* 36 (4): 763–781.
Schumpeter, J.A. 1912. *The theory of economic development: An inquiry into profits, capital, credit, interest, and the business cycle,* 1983 ed., lxiv, 255. Social science classics series. New Brunswick, NJ: Transaction Books.
Shaw, E.S. 1973. *Financial deepening in economic development.* Economic development series, xii, 260. New York: Oxford University Press.
Tsuru, K. 2000. *Finance and growth: Some theoretical considerations and a review of the empirical literature.* Paris: OECD Publishing.
Uygur, E. 1993. *Financial liberalization and economic performance in Turkey,* 24. Ankara: TCMB.
Wijenbergen, V.S. 1991. Credit policy, inflation and growth in a financially repressed economy. *Journal of Development Economics* 13 (1–2): 45–65.
Zirek, D., F. Celebi, and M.K. Hassan. 2016. The islamic banking and economic growth nexus: A panel VAR analysis for Organization of Islamic Cooperation (OIC) countries. *Journal of Economic Cooperation and Development* 37 (1): 69–100.

Authors' Biography

Dr. Selim Demez is Assistant Professor of Political Economics. He got his PhD from Istanbul University. Dr. Demez is still teaching variety of courses in Finance and Economics.

Dr. Hülya Deniz Karakoyun earned her BA and PhD degrees at Istanbul University. Dr. Karakoyun was a visiting scholar at Einaudu

Institute for Economics and Finance, in Rome at 2012. Her research interests include macroeconomics, growth and institutional economics.

Dr. Elif Haykır Hobikoğlu is Associate Professor of Economics. Dr. Hobikoğlu holds PhD in Economics and currently works at Istanbul University. She is teaching variety of courses at the department.

CHAPTER 4

The Turkish Economy and Financing Growth by Dual Banking: Empirical Evidence

Ferda Yerdelen Tatoğlu, Halil Tunalı and Murat Ustaoğlu

Abstract The progress in the industrial revolution in the fields of science and technology led to production methods by attracting investments in the production factors. The change contributed to efficiency of the sectors and to the emergence of sustainable growth. Having resources that will finance new investments offers contribution to the national economy. The conventional model dominates the financial sector in most nations in the world, whereas some nations adopt the IF as an alternative. The presence of the two at the same time is called dual banking system. This study analyses the dynamics of the Turkish economy from a historical perspective, followed by an empirical evaluation of the impact of the CF and the IF in the growth rates with reference to selected real sectors.

Keywords Turkish economy · Development policies · Financing growth

F.Y. Tatoğlu (✉) · H. Tunalı · M. Ustaoğlu
Istanbul University, Istanbul, Turkey
e-mail: yerdelen@istanbul.edu.tr

M. Ustaoğlu and A. İncekara (eds.), *Balancing Islamic and Conventional Banking for Economic Growth*, DOI 10.1007/978-3-319-59554-2_4

Introduction

Brazil and Argentina were two rich countries in the world up until the 1960s after which they became less developed nations as a result of a declining growth rate since 1965 (Altıok and Tuncer 2013). On the other hand, before the industrial revolution, the per capita income of a developed nation was three times greater than the income of at least one developed nation, whereas it is now 60 times greater. These two simple examples indicate that even a slight decline in the annual growth rate will lead to serious changes in the national welfare level in the long run (Pamuk 2015). Growth that dramatically affected the welfare level of the nations has become more visible since World War II. The economic policies of the Western states have become key elements in economic development (Genç 2015).

As the Western world was going through this process of transformation, the Ottoman Empire remained a rural society. A group of intellectuals attempted to devise reformist economic policies for development based on the neoliberal model. The outlook of the world economy through the initial years of the globalization process remained the same (Pamuk 2015). Least developed nations suffered from relatively low growth rates over the centuries due to inability to adapt to the transformation process (Savrul et al. 2013). Developing nations, on the other hand, had been trying to adapt themselves to the process of technological and economic development.

In Italy, Spain and South Korea where liberal policies have been successful in the last 60 years have become developed nations, whereas economic development remained below expectations in countries such as Turkey, Malaysia, Russia, Mexico and Brazil which are now still considered developing countries (Pamuk 2015). This part of the study is focused on the economic policies that served as the foundation of development and growth since the late Ottoman era. The progress and evolution of the finance sector is also reviewed. Finally, the study analyses the impacts of loans offered by CF and IF upon the growth by reliance on empirical methods.

Economic Transition from Ottoman Era to Republic

Turkey is a secular state founded upon the legacy of the Ottoman Empire which serves as a bridge between Europe and Asia. A predominantly Muslim country, Turkey has been governed by a multiparty parliamentary system since the second half of the twentieth century. Because it was established upon the rubrics of the Ottoman Empire, Turkey sought to maintain growth based on modernization. This makes Turkey an interesting case of political and economic development. The economic policies implemented in the past decades, however, failed to meet the expectations. It is necessary to look at the economic policies of the Ottoman Empire in its final years for a proper understanding and analysis of the phases of growth and development in Turkey.

The Ottoman Empire became relatively weaker in comparison to the Western world in the eighteenth century in both military and economic terms. To address the problem, the governing leaders implemented different policies. The European states supported domestic industry and promoted exports, whereas the Ottoman Empire preserved policies that would lead to lack of protection for the domestic industries (Genç 2015). Pamuk (2015) holds that the reason for this is political compromises to the big states of the time including Britain and France to reinstate the state power. But these policies fail to ensure that the government maintains its power. As this was happening, the state also suffered from decline of tax revenues. In addition to Poland, the Ottoman Empire was the only government that was able to collect the least amount of taxes. It is inevitable for a country like this to experience problems in domestic and international security. As a result, the Ottoman Empire encountered serious security problems. To address these problems, the government recognized privileges to powerful states of the time. To this end, the Baltalimanı Trade Agreement adopted in 1818 can be seen as a turning point (Savrul et al. 2013). The agreement featured outward liberal economic policies despite that the state was not ready for competition with the industrialized European states.

The number and amount of the machinery and equipment used in textile has increased. On the other hand, the agricultural needs of the coastal residential areas have been met through imports even if the Ottomans were an agricultural society due to lack of transportation (Pamuk 2015). The Ottoman citizens started to play a less significant role in the economy, whereas the foreigners and aliens have become more significant due to privileges recognized to the European traders over political reasons as well as the low tariff rates (Savrul et al. 2013).

The government held that a weak state would be unable to increase its internal security and military power without ensuring to collect greater amount of taxes. To restore political and military power, the government took short-term measures seeking to increase the tax revenues (Pamuk 2015). However, the wars up to the World War I have done great damage to the economy suffering from structural problems. The vast range of measures including confiscation of properties of the high-level officers and monopolization failed to change the negative course of the developments. As a result, the economy suffered from low growth rates (Kurt et al. 2016).

Some reformist policies have been implemented after the Tanzimat measures through which guarantees were introduced for the lives and properties of all subjects. As part of these reforms, confiscation was ruled out as a measure (Pamuk 2015). The government which was able to interfere with the economy after the war broke out started to implement protectionist policies focused on industrialization (Genç 2015). These policies that were also inherited by the republican regime features the following main pillars (Pamuk 2015):

i. Suspension of capitulation rights and privileges recognized to the foreign traders and investors in an attempt to ensure that the domestic business actors will also become influential.
ii. Ad valorem customs rates applied equally to all goods were lifted and replaced by changing customs rates to ensure that the economy policies will succeed.
iii. The activities of the general debts directorate were abolished and the bonds held by the foreign investors were suspended.

In the 1920s, the economy started to recover through the use of the human and physical capital sources in the country. But despite efforts, the potential has not been fully used. Yet high growth rates were attained in some phases of this period where independent economy policies were pursued.

Growth Policies of Young Republic: Great Depression Era

The economic ability of a country can be measured by its sustainable growth performance. Empirical works give insights on growth models and the dynamics of it; however, they are unable to explain the concept.

For this reason, political decisions by institutional structures should also be included in the growth analyses (Şiriner and Doğru 2005).

The state is the most important political and institutional structure. This general assumption also applies to Turkey as well. Turkey has lost most of its physical and human capital during the war of liberation. The republican government was also aware of the cost associated with the flawed policies in late period of the Ottoman Empire. Therefore, the government decided to revive a national economic model where Muslim-Turkish economic actors were subsidized and supported. In addition, the government also intervened the markets in an attempt to strengthen the private sector (Sönmez 2004). The overall situation before the Great Depression can be described by this general characteristic.

The Great Depression negatively affected Turkish economy. Subsequent to the crisis, many countries implemented neoliberal policies. President Roosevelt introduced radical changes in the US and put the New Deal in place to address the unemployment problem. The single-party government in Turkey took conservative measures against monetary expansion to keep the budget deficit under control. The government mostly implemented statist policies which also inspired some Arab states in the region. In 1934, the government introduced the first 5-year development plan, devised under the influence of the Soviet experience. To attain the goals referred to in the plan, two banks, Sümerbank and Etibank, were established (Pamuk 2015). The plans also proclaimed the economic policies to be implemented that became determinative in the decisions of the economic actors on investment and spending (Kurt et al. 2016).

The government placed priority upon construction of railways and transportation to contribute to the economic capital stock and to build the infrastructure of the country. The industrial facilities constructed by use of state capital manufactured the goods that the private sector needed. The average growth rate through 1929 was maintained at 8.5 *pct*. It significantly dropped to 3.5 *pct* in the aftermath.

The economy was further affected by World War II. The government introduced asset tax to address the budget deficit problem. The non-Muslim minorities were particularly vulnerable in this period since they were forced to pay exorbitant amounts of state tax. However, this did not resolve any major economic problems. The economic problems led to sociological changes which included migration from rural to urban areas. Due to the decline in demand in European countries, the employment in agricultural sector also dropped, leading to serious problems in the urban parts of the country. Bribery and corruption further worsened these problems, causing public resentment (Pamuk 2015). As a result, the single-party government lost the elections in the first multiparty competition.

Economic Policies Implemented in the Process of Membership in NATO

Turkey developed closer ties with the US as a response to the growing threat posed by the Soviet Union which expressed ambitions over Turkish territories. As a part of the rapprochements, Turkey decided to become a member of NATO. In an attempt to show that it is eligible to become part of the Western world, the government introduced measures towards a multiparty regime. In 1950, the first multiparty election was held in Turkey where the Democratic Party came to power. The new government introduced radical changes to the economic policies.

The agenda of the new government was based on placement of priority upon neoliberal policies seeking to implement measures that would minimize the role of the state in the economy. The overall climate in the world permitted the government to follow this path. The US and Western countries have set up institutions to prevent another global crisis and another world war (Pamuk 2015). The main objective of these institutions including the IMF and World Bank was to finance the economic policies of the Western countries through production. Those who wished to use the funds offered by these institutions had to make commitments. Turkey, in this respect, was advised by the World Bank that it should introduce liberal policies to prioritize the improvement of the private sector.

The Korean War, on the other hand, led to price increase in raw materials. A transitional welfare improvement can be observed in countries like Turkey where most of the exports were made up of agricultural products. Improved exports led to fast implementation of the policies that liberalized the import of the consumption goods. As a result, people in the rural areas became relatively prosper. Owing to the funds provided as part of the Marshall Plan enabled the imports of spare parts and other equipment that increased productivity in agricultural sector. The size of agricultural areas has increased significantly in this period (Pamuk 2015). Turkey maintained an average growth rate of 8.7 *pct* in the period between 1947 and 1953. The growth trend contributed to the popularity of the Democratic Party in the elections. Economic conditions started to change after the end of Korean War. A huge decline was observed in the revenues associated with the exporting raw materials.

Currency reserves for imports declined rapidly. The government purchased agricultural products and, at the same time, offered credits to subsidize to the agricultural sector. Decreasing reserve level in the state-owned banks led to an increased inflation rate of 15 *pct*. The workers and public servants became disgruntled due to the growing inflation rate. Because imports declined substantially, the domestic manufacturers started to produce the previously imported goods and materials. Most of the resources were allocated to the development of domestic industry. Approval by State Planning Organization (SPO) was made obligatory for the release of loans to the private sector. But the Justice Party altered the structure and composition of the SPO after the coup in a way to implement its populist policies. As a result, SPO implemented economic policies that placed emphasis upon the short term needs of the private sector instead of long-term policies. In some sectors, import was strictly forbidden to protect the domestic producers. This led to a hybrid industrial production model in both public and private sectors.

The world economy grew significantly in the period between 1944 and 1970. A similar trend was also observed in Turkey in the same period. This had reflections in the improved per capita income level. As a result of this, the investments constituted 12 *pct* of the GDP in 1950 and 20 *pct* in 1970. Most of these investments have been financed by domestic savings (Pamuk 2015). The economic policies have been revised occasionally; but the nationalist and protectionist policies have been preserved up to the early 1980s when structural transformation policies were first implemented.

Post-Keynesian Era and Liberalization

A short history of sustainable development reveals that the Western countries have been very stable, whereas Muslim countries have not. Turkey is the only Muslim country that has been ranked among the top 20 economies in the world despite its unstable performance in the global development race. Compared to other countries in the region, Turkey was able to modernize its economy thanks to the economic development plans implemented in the late Ottoman period (Şimşek 2007). The structural transformation of the economy that took place in the 1980s contributed a great deal to this success. The short- and mid-term economic development plans should be reviewed to better understand the growth performance of the economy. Even though neoliberal policies had been integrated with the overall economic approach of the 1980s, the planning never ceased (Şiriner and Doğru 2005). However, in the planning stage, much focus was paid to labour efficiency and manufacturing industry with higher added value (Altıok and Tuncer 2013).

In 1980s, the overall situation in the world started to change; under the leadership of Ronald Reagan in the US and Margaret Thatcher in UK, neoliberal policies replaced Keynesian policies because of the belief that state involvement in the economy was detrimental to economic performance (Pamuk 2015). The protectionist barriers were removed and inspections of international capital movements were made less frequent (Karaçor 2006). Developing nations were also advised by the IMF and the World Bank to follow the same path (Şiriner and Doğru 2005). However, they did not show a strong interest in neoliberal policies because they had not yet completed the process of development and structural transformation. Yet they were unable to resist IMF policies because they lacked sufficient domestic resources to finance investments (Pamuk 2015). As a result, a transformation process where neoliberal policies were implemented started in the developing economies.

But the neoliberal policies were suspended in Turkey in the 1990s due to the crises and recession associated with the political turmoil. However, since the 2000s, Turkey has been able to maintain a high growth rate allowing it to become one of the G20 nations. According to Pamuk (2015), the relative success should be attributed to Turkey's decisiveness to follow the overall trend in the global economy. Chronologically speaking, the open economic model of the nineteenth century was replaced by a protectionist industrial model in the first half of the twentieth century. In the aftermath of the 1980s, on the other hand, neoliberal policies focusing on free markets were implemented (Öztürk and Özyakışır 2005). The political instability in the 1970s and the growing problems made it impossible to pursue import-oriented policies. The 24 January decisions taken by the military administration that came to power after a military coup in 1980 are considered a turning point in the history of Turkey's economy. The decisions mainly sought to ensure structural transformation for further exports and a competitive economy (Kibritçioğlu 2001). The positive contribution of exporting based on the production of goods and services is called the export-oriented growth hypothesis (Şimşek 2003).

Policies of liberalization for financial capital to ensure entry of foreign capital as well as devaluation of the local currency in an attempt to address budget deficits were implemented. The currency rates, under this scheme, were determined on a daily basis. Public incentives were lifted to decrease the amount of public losses. Private sector was supported to increase and promote exports. To this end, exporters were recognized some privileges including tax reduction and currency incentives. In 1983, the patrons of the 24 January decisions came to power in the first elections after the military coup. The new administration was able to reduce the inflation rate from 90 to 40 *pct.* However, this threshold has not been exceeded due to significant budget deficits associated with public expenditures (Pamuk 2015). Yet the country attracted foreign capital and investment because of the government's neoliberal policies and the prime minister's close ties with the IMF and the World Bank.

Some additional changes were introduced under the liberalization policies for a number of financial transactions that were previously performed by the central bank. The priority was to integrate with the world economy and transform the economy into a more competitive one. It was not possible to attain these goals by state-owned enterprises. For this reason, the government further introduced policies to strengthen private sector. However, the privatization of state-owned enterprises poses some problems. Due to the mistakes in this process, the public refrained from extending support to the measures. In the 1991 elections, the ruling party lost as a result of these mistakes. The most important success of the 1980s was the rise in exports. Turkey has become the country that increased its exports the most among developing nations. The private sector which was unable to compete with the rest of the world due to the government incentives did not support the neoliberal policies at first. This remained the case up to the 2000s. On the other hand, despite major problems including inflation, unemployment and income inequality, the 1980s raised hopes for welfare. But the 1990s became one of the most notorious phases of the republican era in economic terms (Karagöl 2013).

A coalition government was formed after the elections in 1991, starting the era of populist and unstable coalition governments (Karagöl 2013). These coalition governments were visibly unsuccessful in their economic policies, leaving a legacy of major problems for the next generations (Karaçor 2006). The privatization of state-owned enterprises stopped while state incentives for unproductive sectors were reinstated. The retirement age was reduced to 38, causing a danger of bankruptcy in the social security system. A review of the macro indicators in the 1990s reveals that the economy was not in good shape during this period.

Yet apart from these problems, the most important economic development in this period was the creation of the Customs Union agreement in 1996 with the European Union. Under the agreement, the parties sought to reduce customs gradually. The policies supporting the structural transformation process were revised and implemented (Togan 2015). Additionally, Turkey committed itself to reducing the customs rates with the third countries to the rates applicable to the EU (Pamuk 2015).

In the 2000s, problems emerged due to the fact that the EU moved from the CU to the free trade agreements in its foreign trade policies. Turkey, without being admitted as a full member, had to comply with the provisions of the FTAs that the EU concluded with a number of countries in different parts of the world. The EU signed FTAs with South Korea and Latin America; similar arrangements were also expected with respect to Japan, China, Canada and the US in the future. Currently, the parties are reviewing the content and provisions of the Customs Union agreement that have worked in disfavour of Turkey over the past decades. In the initial years of the CU, exports to the EU remained almost the same; but with the accelerated technology transfer and diversification of investments, the manufacturing industry has become particularly competitive. The automotive and white goods industries have performed the most successful exports in the subsequent decades.

The 1990s are remembered as the lost years of the nation due to the economic failures in this period. In 2001, a huge crisis erupted, culminating in an election victory of the AK Party (Acar 2013). The new government enjoyed a remarkable parliamentary support. Acemoğlu and Ucer (2002) upheld that the national economy grew rapidly in the period between 2002 and 2007, the most successful era of the entire republican era. The success of the AK Party government in the field of economy led to growing political support. The growing popular support for the AK Party government can be attributed to the successful economic policies (Seval and Özdemir 2013). But in fact, the policies they were implementing were the revised versions of the neoliberal policies from the Özal era.

According to Derviş (2013) Turkey performed better than many other countries in the world including the EU members. The GDP which declined to 168 billion USD in 2001 grew to 799 billion in 2014. The amount of exports, on the other hand, increased from 2.9 billion USD in 1980 to 31 billion in 2001 and to 157 billion in 2014. Pragmatist decisions were made in a number of issues on the economy. For instance, the radical decisions by Kemal Derviş, appointed as Minister of Economy by the coalition government after the 2001 economic crisis, were implemented with only slight revisions. Derviş's Transition to Strong Economy Programme, composed of foreign trade and currency policy, fiscal policy, anti-inflation policy and structural reform policies, was put in place (Şimşek 2007). The AK Party government maintained stability, contributing a great deal to the economic indicators (Öniş 2012). Despite the global economic crisis in 2008, Turkey maintained 5.1 *pct* of annual growth rate, being ranked as the fastest growing economy in the world in the decade (Derviş 2013). As a result of stability in the economy, the inflation rate declined to one-digit figures. Growth, on the other hand, remained stable even though it was affected by some domestic and external developments.

The AK Party first took measures to rebuild confidence in markets (Karagöl 2013). The measures worked well, reducing the budget deficits. The resulting positive mood also affected other sectors, removing the traces of the crisis (Derviş 2013). As the public need for borrowing declined, inflation rate as well as the interest rates declined. The share of the interest expenditures in the budget among the total spending was 40 *pct* in 2004, declining to 13 *pct* in 2012 (Seval and Özdemir 2013). In the initial years of its office term, the AK Party government made efforts towards EU membership (Öniş 2012). However, despite bold performance in the field of economy, the negotiations did not result in full membership which disappointed the public and raised skepticism about the sincerity of the EU. Amid negotiations, Germany and France expressed that they were opposed to Turkey's membership. Despite the ongoing talks, no full membership of Turkey in the EU is expected in the near future (Yıldırım and Dura 2007).

One of the problems that negatively affect growth in the developing economies like the one in Turkey is insufficient capital accumulation. This slows down the technological renewal process in export-intensive sectors. For this reason, export-based development strategy is implemented to support private sector initiatives. To ensure that the manufacturing industry becomes competitive, policies for a greater amount of foreign capital were implemented. This measure worked; as a result, manufacturing industry has grown by 7 *pct* on average in the period between 1991 and 2007 (Altıok and Tuncer 2013).

Turkey's growth performance was better than South America, Africa, Middle East and many Asian nations in the Second World War. It lagged behind Italy, Japan, South Korea and some southern European countries (Pamuk 2015). In general, the overall economic trend in the world was pursued. The success in development and stability in sustainable growth makes structural transformation necessary. So far, the economic policies implemented since the late Ottoman period have been reviewed to better analyse the growth policies. Before empirical analysis, it is useful to evaluate the financial sector that provides funds for the growth.

Agriculture Industry

Most parts of Turkey are suitable for agricultural activities. The agricultural practices and engagements constituted a major part of the economy in the Saljuki and Ottoman eras. Historical records indicate that 80–90 *pct* of the public revenues were based on agricultural activities during the Ottoman era. The main agricultural activities included production of wheat, cotton, tobacco, fruits and vegetables (Yavuz and Çağlayan 2005). The policies implemented in this field in the republican era have, however, varied. Initially, it was financially supported because the administration held that agriculture was a sector that would ensure development. Different institutions were set up to add an institutional identity to the sector. These institutions were mainly charged with performing in favour of the agriculture actors and providing incentives. However, most of the public incentives were lifted after the 24 January decisions. In the 1990s, the policies were revisited again. The significance of the sector became clear in the membership talks with the EU (Benek 2007). Three of the 35 negotiation chapters were directly (and nine indirectly) relevant to the agricultural sector.

It could be argued that the sector indirectly contributed to the financial sector because it was one of the reasons for the establishment of the largest bank in the country. In 1863, Homeland Offices were set up to provide loans for the farmers. But the system was shortly liquidated due to growing corruption, being replaced by a similar initiative. When similar problems erupted, Ziraat Bank, the largest in the country, was founded in the form of a conventional bank (Yetiz 2016). The bank is currently the most important institution that provides funds for the agriculture sector. The bank's mission also includes regulating the executive structures of the agricultural loan cooperatives. Both CF and IF systems offer financial products for the financial needs of the agriculture sector. Despite this, the share of the agriculture sector within the economy has declined over the time due to mistakes and unstable, populist and short-term policies.

Manufacturing Industry

The history of manufacturing in Turkey can be traced back to the Ottoman era which experienced the repercussions of the industrial revolution because it significantly lagged behind Europe in terms of industrial development. The total size of the industrial institutions in Turkey in the Ottoman era was 20 k horsepower, whereas it was 210 k in Britain. The figures clearly indicate that the Ottoman economy suffered extremely from the lack of industrialization (Akyıldız and Eroğlu 2004).

The first decade of the republican regime which allowed private enterprises is the initial part of the liberal era in Turkey (Doğan 2013). Despite that the government wanted to increase the share of the private sector in the industry, the capital structure was not suitable for doing this. To provide interim goods for the private sector enterprises, state-owned enterprises were created in different parts of the country. Investments were made in a number of sectors including finance and sugar production. But with the eruption of World War II, conservative and protectionist policies were adopted, reducing the size of investments. Accompanied by declining demand due to stagnation in global economy, the size of the manufacturing industry shrank. A second liberalization period started with the change of economic policies in 1950 when the first democratically elected government came to power. The government set up private industrial institutions in Istanbul, Ankara, Izmir and Adana. The manufacturing industry attracted investments in the 1960s owing to the attention paid to the sector in the 5-year development plans. However, industrialization slowed down up until the 1980s because of the lack of significant amounts of foreign investment.

The radical change in economic policies in the 1980s led to accelerated industrialization process. The export-oriented development policies reduced the size of agricultural sector, whereas the manufacturing industry has become popular in this era, attracting greater amount of public incentives. The sector tended to rely on exports due to the domestic crises in the 1990s. A radical transformation was experienced in the productivity of the manufacturing industry thanks to the growing technology transfer after the CU. The reforms introduced in the 2000s increased the size of foreign trade and the productivity of the manufacturing industry.

Considering the contribution of the sector upon growth and national welfare, it becomes clear that it is important to implement policies in support of the sector activities. For this reason, the remaining parts of the study are focused on the empirical analysis of the relationship between the financing of the real sector and the financial capital to ensure that the economy maintains higher growth rates.

Empirical Analysis

To analyse the potential impacts of the funds provided by IF and CF institutions in Turkey to the sectors upon the Gross National Product (GDP), this study uses the seemingly unrelated regression method. After explaining the variables and data used in the econometric analysis, the study analyses the econometric method and the findings.

Variables and Data

The data on the variables provided below have been compiled from the TCMB[1] and BDDK[2] for the period between 2005: 1 and 2015: 3. The series were first seasonally adjusted and the logarithms of the series were also taken (Table 4.1).

Table 4.1 Variables used in the econometric analysis

Variable	*Meaning*
lngdp	GDP
lnagriculture	Loans offered by CF institutions for agriculture
lnconstruction	Loans offered by CF institutions for construction
lnmining	Loans offered by CF institutions for mining
lnmanufacturing	Loans offered by CF institutions for manufacturing
lntourism	Loans offered by CF institutions for tourism
lnisagriculture	Loans offered by IF institutions for agriculture
lnisconstruction	Loans offered by IF institutions for construction
lnismining	Loans offered by IF institutions for mining
lnismanufacturing	Loans offered by IF institutions for manufacturing
lnistourism	Loans offered by IF institutions for tourism

Econometric Method

This study employs seemingly unrelated regression (SUR), developed by Zellner and Pagan (1962). The SUR models are based on the simultaneous analysis of the multi-equational models. Unlike simultaneous equations system, these models do not involve endogenous variable in the right side of the equations; all variables are included as exogenous ones. For two equations and two independent variables, a SUR equation can be denoted as follows:

$$Y_{2t} = \beta_{12} + \beta_{22}X_{2t} + \beta_{32}Z_{2t} + e_2 \tag{4.1}$$

$$Y_{2t} = \beta_{12} + \beta_{22}X_{2t} + \beta_{32}Z_{2t} + e_2 \tag{4.2}$$

The equations here are seemingly unrelated; however, the error terms of the equations are related. Zellner and Pagan (1962), in this case, shows that use of SUR which takes into account the correlation of residuals is a best option. The estimation of the SUR model is performed by generalized least squares (GLS) produce efficient estimator than the OLS.

If there is no relation between the residuals of the equations, the SUR analysis will have no precedence over the OLS. For this reason, the significance of the correlation between the residuals is reviewed and analysed. To analyse the correlation between the residuals, there are a number of tests in the literature, the most notable one being the Breusch and Pagan (1979) Lagrange Multiplier (LM) test. The main hypothesis of the test suggests that the covariance between the residuals is zero; the alternative hypothesis, on the other hand, stresses that at least one covariance is not zero. In a system of the two equations given above, for a simultaneous correlation test, the H_0 and H_1 hypotheses can be denoted as follows:

$$\begin{aligned} H_0 &: \sigma_{12} = 0 \\ H_1 &: \sigma_{12} \neq 0 \end{aligned} \tag{4.3}$$

σ_{12} is the covariance between e_1 and e_2, whereas T is the number of observations, M is the number of equations and r_{ij} is the correlation between the residuals of the different equations. The LM test statistic can be calculated as follows:

$$\lambda = T \sum_{i=1}^{M} \sum_{j=1}^{i-1} r_{ij}^2 \tag{4.4}$$

LM test has χ^2 distribution with the degree of freedom $M(M\text{-}1)/2$. If main hypothesis is rejected, it is assumed that there is relation between residuals and that the use of the SUR model is appropriate.

Econometric Analysis

Before econometric analysis, correlation matrixes were set up to analyse the correlations between loans offered by CF and IF institutions by sectors and the GDP. To this end, the graphs of the variables were also evaluated.

A review of the correlation matrixes in Tables 4.2 and 4.3 reveal that the loans offered by CF and IF for the sectors have a positive, strong and significant relationship with the GDP. In addition, the loans for the sectors had high and significant correlation among themselves.

Such high correlations between independent variables lead to a problem of multi-collinearity which represents a deviation from an important

Table 4.2 The correlation matrix between the loans offered by CF institutions by sectors and the GDP

	lngdp	*lnagriculture*	*lnconstruction*	*lnmining*	*lnmanufacturing*	*lntourism*
lngdp	1.0000					
lnagriculture	0.9837	1.0000				
lnconstruction	0.9943	0.9797	1.0000			
lnmining	0.9847	0.9769	0.9900	1.0000		
lnmanufacturing	0.9966	0.9842	0.9975	0.9904	1.0000	
lntourism	0.9926	0.9843	0.9976	0.9948	0.9962	1.0000

Table 4.3 The correlation matrix between the loans offered by IF institutions by sectors and the GDP

	lngdp	*lnisagriculture*	*lnisconstruction*	*lnismining*	*lnismanufacturing*	*lnistourism*
lngdp	1.0000					
lnisagriculture	0.9621	1.0000				
lnisconstruction	0.9466	0.9499	1.0000			
lnismining	0.9094	0.9087	0.8659	1.0000		
Lnismanufacturing	0.9615	0.9776	0.9894	0.8778	1.0000	
lnistourism	0.9445	0.9485	0.9845	0.8851	0.9776	1.0000

assumption of OLS, affecting the efficiency of the econometric estimations. Therefore, including these independent variables into the same regression model will lead to biased parameter estimations; for this reason, it will be more suitable to employ separate models to see the net impacts. In addition to the correlations referred to above, a correlation between the residuals of the two regressions to look for the impact of the loans by the CF and the IF institutions to the sectors upon the GDP is also expected.

$$\begin{aligned} \text{lngdp}_t &= \alpha_0 + \alpha_1 \text{lnagriculture}_t + u_t \\ \text{lngdp}_t &= \beta_0 + \beta_1 \text{lnisagriculture}_t + v_t \end{aligned}$$

The residuals out of the two models above were processed via Breusch and Pagan (1979) LM test to test the correlation between $\hat{u}_t$ and $\hat{v}_t$, and the results were presented at the bottom of the Tables (4.4, 4.5, 4.6, 4.7, 4.8). The results indicate that the correlations for most sectors are high. To ignore this correlation will lead to a biased parameters estimation. For this reason, seemingly unrelated regression was employed to consider the correlation between the residuals.

The correlation between the residuals of the regressions maintained between the loans offered by CF and IF institutions to the construction sector and the GDP is 46 *pct*; and according to the Breusch and Pagan LM test, the correlation is significant, revealing that the use of the SUR model was appropriate. The SUR model results indicate that a 1 *pct* increase in the loans by the CF institutions for the construction sector

Table 4.4 SUR estimation for relationship between loans by CF–IF institutions for construction sector and GDP

lngdp		*lngdp*		
Constant	12.5382[a]	Constant	14.0147[a]	
lnconstruction	0.4019[a]	lnisconstruction	0.3276[a]	
R^2	0.9883	R^2	0.8959	
χ^2	3591.26[a]	χ^2	359.31[a]	
Correlation matrix			$\hat{u}_t$	$\hat{v}_t$
		$\hat{u}_t$	1.0000	
		$\hat{v}_t$	0.4590	1.0000
Breusch Pagan LM test		8.810[a]		

Note [a]Denotes significance at the level of 1%

Table 4.5 OLS estimation for relationship between loans by CF and IF institutions for agriculture sector and GDP

lngdp		*lngdp*		
Constant	10.9539[a]	Constant		10.6272[a]
lnagriculture	0.4771[a]	lnisagriculture		0.6164[a]
R^2	0.9677	R^2		0.9257
F	1197.4[a]	F		498.18[a]
Correlation matrix			$\hat{u}_t$	$\hat{v}_t$
		$\hat{u}_t$	1.0000	
		$\hat{v}_t$	−0.1182	1.0000
Breusch Pagan LM test		0.587		

Note [a]Denotes significance at the level of 1%

Table 4.6 SUR estimation for relationship between loans by CF–IF institutions for manufacturing sector and GDP

lngdp		*lngdp*		
Constant	8.3423[a]	Constant		9.2384[a]
lnmanufacturing	0.5674[a]	lnismanufacturing		0.5926[a]
R^2	0.9930	R^2		0.9244
χ^2	6055.59[a]	χ^2		512.48[a]
Correlation matrix			$\hat{u}_t$	$\hat{v}_t$
		$\hat{u}_t$	1.0000	
		$\hat{v}_t$	0.4516	1.0000
Breusch Pagan LM test		8.566[a]		

Note [a]Denotes significance at the level of 1%

increase the GDP by 0.40 *pct*, whereas this becomes approximately 0.33 *pct* in the case of the IF institutions.

The Breusch and Pagan (1979) LM test results reveal that the correlation between the residuals of the regressions between the loans by CF and IF institutions for the agricultural sector and the GDP is not significant. In this case, it will be appropriate to estimate the models through OLS separately. The OLS results reveal that a 1 *pct* increase in the loans by CF institutions for the agricultural sector increases the GDP by approximately 0.48 *pct*, whereas a 1 *pct* increase in the loans offered by IF institutions for the sector increase it by 0.62 *pct* approximately.

The Breusch and Pagan (1979) LM test results reveal that the correlation between the residuals of the regressions between the loans by CF and IF institutions for the manufacturing industry and the GDP is

Table 4.7 SUR estimation for relationship between loans by CF and IF institutions for tourism sector and GDP

lngdp		*lngdp*		
Constant	12.0446[a]	Constant		14.3083[a]
lntourism	0.4038[a]	lnistourism		0.3675[a]
R^2	0.9852	R^2		0.8925
χ^2	2780.93[a]	χ^2		344.04[a]
Correlation matrix			$\hat{u}_t$	$\hat{v}_t$
		$\hat{u}_t$	1.0000	
		$\hat{v}_t$	0.3405	1.0000
Breusch Pagan LM test		4.871[b]		

Note [a]and [b]Denote significance at the levels of 1% and 5% respectively

Table 4.8 OLS estimation for relationship between CF and IF loans for mining sector and GDP

lngdp		*lngdp*		
Constant	12.1876[a]	Constant		8.2016[a]
lnmining	0.4375[a]	lnismining		0.7551[a]
R^2	0.9697	R^2		0.8269
F	1279.74[a]	F		191.13[a]
Correlation matrix			$\hat{u}_t$	$\hat{v}_t$
		$\hat{u}_t$	1.0000	
		$\hat{v}_t$	−0.2017	1.0000
Breusch Pagan LM test		1.708		

Note [a]Denotes significance at the level of 1%

significant (45 *pct*). SUR model results reveal that a 1 *pct* increase in the loans by CF institutions for the manufacturing sector increases the GDP by 0.57 *pct* approximately, whereas a 1 *pct* increase in the loans offered by IF institutions for the sector increase it by 0.59 *pct*.

The correlation between the residuals of the regressions between the loans by CF and IF institutions for the tourism sector and the GDP is significant (34 *pct*). SUR model results reveal that a 1 *pct* increase in the loans by CF institutions for the tourism sector increases the GDP by 0.40 *pct*, whereas a 1 *pct* increase in the loans offered by IF institutions for the sector increases it by 0.37 *pct* approximately.

Test results indicate that the correlation between the residuals of the regressions between the loans by CF and IF institutions for the mining industry and the GDP is not significant. The OLS results reveal that a

1 *pct* increase in the loans by CF institutions for the mining sector increases the GDP by approximately 0.44 *pct*, whereas a 1 *pct* increase in the loans offered by IF institutions for the sector increase it by 0.76 *pct* approximately.

Notes

1. The Central Bank of Turkey.
2. Turkish Banking Regulation and Supervision Agency.

References

Acar, F. 2013. Türkiye Ekonomisine Genel Bakış (2001–2013). *ÇSGB Çalışma Dünyası Dergisi* 1 (2): 1532.

Acemoğlu, D., and M. Ucer. 2015. The ups and downs of Turkish growth, 2002–2015: Political dynamics, the European Union and the institutional slide. In *NBER Working Paper*. The National Bureau of Economic Research.

Akyıldız, H., and Ö. Eroğlu. 2004. Türkiye Cumhuriyeti dönemi uygulanan iktisat politikaları. *Süleyman Demirel Üniversitesi İktisadi ve İdari Bilimler Fakültesi Dergisi* 9 (1): 43–62.

Altıok, M., and İ. Tuncer. 2013. Türkiye imalat sanayinde yapısal değişim ve üretkenlik: 1980–2008 Dönemi. *Anadolu Üniversitesi Sosyal Bilimler Dergisi* 13 (2): 55–70.

Benek, S. 2007. *Avrupa Birliği'ne uyum sürecinde Türkiye'deki tarımsal işletmelerin günümüzdeki durumu.* Marmara Coğrafya Dergisi. 15: 191–206.

Breusch, T., and A. Pagan. 1979. A simple test of heteroskedasticity and random coefficient variation. *Econometrica* 47: 1287–1294.

Derviş, K. 2013. Turkey and Europe: A new perspective. In *Global Turkey in Europe: Political, economic, and foreign policy dimensions of Turkey's evolving relationship with the EU*, ed. S. Aydın-Düzgit, 21–31. Roma: Edizioni Nuova Cultura.

Doğan, M. 2013. A general outlook on the industrialization process of Turkey. *Marmara Coğrafya Dergisi* 28 (2): 211–231.

Genç, M. 2015. *Osmanlı İmparatorluğu'nda Devlet ve Ekonomi*, 12th ed. Ötüken Neşriyat: İstanbul.

Karaçor, Z. 2006. Öğrenen ekonomi Türkiye: Kasım 2000-Şubat 2001 krizinin öğrettikleri. *Selçuk Üniversitesi Sosyal Bilimler Enstitüsü Dergisi* 16 (1): 379–391.

Karagöl, E.T., A.S. Bingöl, and Ü.İ. Mıhçıokur. 2013. *Ak Parti Dönemi Türkiye Ekonomisi*,, ed. E.T. Karagöl. Ankara: SETA.

Karagöl, E.T. 2013. The Turkish economy during the justice and development party decade. *Insight Turkey* 15 (4): 115–129.

Kibritçioğlu, A. 2001. Türkiye'de ekonomik krizler ve hükümetler, 1969–2001, 1–18. *Yeni Türkiye Dergisi*, Özel Sayı.
Kurt, M., B. Çakır, and K. Demir. 2016. Türkiye'de modern yönetimin erken dönemleri: Geç-Osmanlı döneminde fabrikalar, sanayi mektepleri ve yabancı uzmanlar. *Istanbul University Journal of the School of Business* 45 (Special Issue): 154–165.
Öniş, Z. 2012. The triumph of conservative globalism: The political economy of the AKP era. *Turkish Studies* 13 (2): 135–152.
Öztürk, S., and D. Özyakışır. 2005. Türkiye ekonomisinde 1980 sonrası yaşanan yapısal dönüşümlerin GSMH, dış ticaret ve dış borçlar bağlamında teorik bir değerlendirmesi. *Mevzuat Dergisi* 94 (8): 2–18.
Pamuk, Ş. 2015. *Türkiye'nin 200 Yıllık İktisadi Tarihi*, 5. Baskı, 377. İstanbul: Türkiye İş Bankası Kültür Yayınları.
Savrul, B.K., H.A. Özel, and C. Kılıç. 2013. Osmanlı'nın son döneminden günümüze Türkiye'de dış ticaretin gelişimi. *Journal of Entrepreneurship and Development* 8 (1): 55–79.
Seval, B., and A.K. Özdemir. 2013. *2000'li Yıllardan Günümüze Değişen Türkiye Ekonomis*, 3–25. İstanbul: SERPAM.
Şimşek, M. 2003. İhracata dayalı büyüme hipotezinin Türkiye ekonomisi verileri ile analizi, 1960–2002. *Dokuz Eylül Üniversitesi İktisadi ve İdari Bilimler Fakültesi Dergisi* 18 (2): 43–63.
Şimşek, H.A. 2007. Türkiye'de 2000 sonrasında uygulanan istikrar programlarının kamu maliyesine etkileri. *Finans Politik & Ekonomik Yorumlar* 44 (512): 52–69.
Şiriner, İ., and Y. Doğru. 2005. Türkiye ekonomisinin büyüme dinamikleri üzerine bir değerlendirme. *Yönetim Bilimleri Dergisi* 3 (2): 162–183.
Sönmez, M. 2004. *Türkiye Ekonomisinin 80 yılı*, 200. İstanbul: Istanbul Ticaret Odası.
Togan, S. 2015. The EU-Turkey customs union: A model for future Euro-Med integration. In *Economic and social development of the Southern and Eastern Mediterranean countries*, ed. R. Ayadi, M. Dabrowski, and L. De Wulf, 37–48. Cham: Springer International Publishing.
Yavuz, F., and T. Çağlayan. 2005. Türkiye tarımının tarihi. In *Türkiye'de Tarım*, ed. F. Yavuz, 1–8. Ankara: Tarım ve Köyişleri Bakanlığı.
Yetiz, F. 2016. Bankacılığın doğuşu ve Türk bankacılık sistemi. *Niğde Üniversitesi İktisadi ve İdari Bilimler Fakültesi Dergisi* 9 (2): 107–120.
Yıldırım, E., and C. Dura. 2007. Gümrük Birliğinin Türkiye ekonomisi üzerindeki etkileri konusundaki literatüre bir bakış. *Erciyes Üniversitesi İktisadi ve İdari Bilimler Fakültesi Dergisi* 28: 141–177.
Zellner, A., and A. Pagan. 1962. An efficient method of estimating seemingly unrelated regressions and tests for aggregation bias. *Journal of the American Statistical Association* 57 (298): 348–368.

Authors' Biography

Dr. Ferda Yerdelen Tatoğlu is Associate Professor of Econometrics at Istanbul University. She was born and educated in Turkey, and served as visiting scholar at University of Leicester Department of Economics. Dr. Tatoğlu is most recently the author of "Introductory Econometrics A Modern Approach" (2013), "İleri Panel Veri Analizi" (2012), "Panel Veri Ekonometrisi"(2012), and many other research in economics and econometrics.

Dr. Halil Tunalı is Associate Professor of Economics. He received his BA, MA and PhD degrees in Economics from Istanbul University. Dr. Tunalı who also delivers lectures at the Foundation of Science and Art teaches introductory and advanced courses in the field of economics andfinance.

Dr. Murat Ustaoğlu is an Associate Professor of Islamic Economics. He was born in Turkey, and educated at the Ramapo College of New Jersey (B.A.) and the City University of New York (M.A.), and holds a Ph.D. degree in Economics. Dr. Ustaoğlu has worked at Bank of New York and JP Morgan Chase Bank in US. He is, most recently, co-author of Islamic Finance Alternatives for Emerging Economies (2014), Post-Conflict Syrian State and Nation Building (2015) and many research articles focusing Islamic Finance and Economics. Additionally, he teaches undergraduate and graduate level various courses in Economics.

CHAPTER 5

Financing Economic Growth by Dual Banking in Malaysia: Empirical Evidence

Mehmet Akyol, Ferda Yerdelen Tatoğlu and Murat Ustaoğlu

Abstract The performances of the commanding height sectors including agriculture, manufacturing, construction, tourism and mining are crucially important for growth. To improve the productivity and competitiveness of these sectors, it is imperative to offer financial options and opportunities. Despite that Malaysia gained its independence recently, the country experienced a fairly satisfactory level of development. The contribution of the financial sector greatly influenced the success of the policies that offered solutions to the structural problems of Malaysia's economy. For this reason, the Malaysian government has taken steps to improve the CF and IF. The stability of both sectors enables scholars to run a comparative analysis. This study seeks to provide a comparative analysis of growth based on empirical measurements of the impact of loans offered by conventional and Islamic finance.

Keywords Malaysian economy · Financing growth · Islamic finance

M. Akyol (✉) · F.Y. Tatoğlu · M. Ustaoğlu
Istanbul University, Istanbul, Turkey
e-mail: makyol@gumushane.edu.tr

M. Ustaoğlu and A. İncekara (eds.), *Balancing Islamic and Conventional Banking for Economic Growth*, DOI 10.1007/978-3-319-59554-2_5

Introduction

Malaysia is one of the countries that developed successful solutions to the social and economic issues in the Muslim world. Malaysia gained its independence in 1948 and is a federal state composed of 13 provinces inclusive of nearly 18,000 islands. It is a parliamentary democracy with a federal constitutional monarchy and comprises three main ethnic groups: Malays, Chinese and Indians (Subramaniam et al. 2014). Diversity runs deep even among these different ethnic groups.

Traces of Malaysia's colonial past can be observed in the economy and in other fields. Europeans played a huge role in the national economy before the independence. In the initial years, the country has remained an agricultural actor with low level of income. In the 1970s, the industrial sector also emerged, causing the country to enjoy rapid economic development and growth (Yusof 2008).

According to the growth reports published in 2008, Malaysia is one of 13 countries to secure an average growth rate of 7*pct* in the last 25 years. It can also be argued that the country was able to deal with poverty very successfully in that period. In 1960s, more than half of the population was under the poverty line, whereas this figure is currently only 1*pct*. These successes are a direct result of the long-term economic policies implemented by the government. Currently, the Malaysian economy is in good shape, with a low inflation rate and an average growth rate of 7*pct*.

The success of the economic policies in Malaysia's history can be attributed to its performance in three stages: New Economic Policy (NEP) in the period between 1970 and 1990, National Development Policy (NDP) in the period between 1990 and 2000 and the National Vision Policy (NVP) in the period between 2001 and 2010. These policies played a monumental role in attaining growth and development goals, and also contributed to the solution of many social problems in the country. In this section of the study, Malaysia's economic policies and the role of the different sectors in these policies will be analysed. In the final section, the study will empirically evaluate how conventional and Islamic financial systems provide financial needs for the real sector.

The Economic Policies

In theory, growth is considered to be a process where a number of factors interact with each other. Even in the most basic models, a number of new variables are added or removed in the growth process analyses.

For this reason, economists who focus on developing countries agree that certain dynamic factors play a role in the growth and development processes (Kogid et al. 2010). The impact of the dynamic factors on the economy is observed more visibly in developing nations like Malaysia. In the initial years of Malaysia's economy, agriculture was important. Subsequently, the economy went through a process of structural transformation in the 1990s from industrialization to a knowledge economy. However, the decisive and successful economic policies are not limited to the growth and industrialization (Yusof 2008). In the process of drafting these policies, social problems including ethnic discrimination, unfair income distribution and poverty were also taken into consideration. It could be argued that the general framework of the import-substitution industrialization policy was implemented shortly before the independence. As in other colonies, the general role attributed to Malaysia in the colonial era was to serve as a market for industrial products and to provide raw materials for the British industry. Local actors and capital holders handled the technical infrastructure projects, as long as these services were provided (Jomo 2006).

Economic policies designed with the consideration of Malaysia's fast development played a huge role in the country's success. The first step of this success story was a 5-year development plan implemented in 1969 called The National Economic Policy (NEP). These policies contributed to the rapid development of the country and also addressed pressing social problems. The first development plan was implemented in the aftermath of class clashes in 1969 when socioeconomic restructuring was identified as a main target. In essence, the plan sought to address class discrimination and alleviate the impact of poverty (Leong 1992). As part of this plan, measures were taken to ensure that locals would get employment in the administration and real sector and enjoy socioeconomic rights (Tan 2014). These policies, implemented through a period of two decades, seem to be successful as locals were employed more frequently in the real and public sectors. The successful results of these policies also include the growing role of the manufacturing sector in the economy. The export-based development model contributed to a process of transformation in employment. The employment rate in the manufacturing sector in 1957 was 5.2*pct*, whereas it became 20.1*pct* in 1991. The share of manufacturing in the exports rose from 27.5*pct* in 1971 to 36.6*pct* in 1989 (Jomo 2006). Despite this trend, however, the manufacturing industry did not improve sufficiently in this period. Yet, it contributed to social welfare in general.

The removal of class discrimination in economic activities improved the income level of residence in cities, and the life standards of people in rural areas (Milne 1976). The share of public capital in investments that contribute to sectors such as the manufacturing industry in developing countries (like Malaysia) is very important (Jomo 2006). Following the initial policies, The National Development Policy (NDP) developed as an extension of the NEP, but with some modifications and innovations. The NDP mainly sought to address poverty and participation of locals in economic activities. Additionally, it focused on the human capital to attain goals of fair income distribution and sustainable growth. Strategies which developed as part of the NDP included innovative policies of agricultural sector, infrastructural supports, professional activities, introduction of charity funds and ceiling price practices performed in line with the interaction of the market players for price stability (Bank 2004). The 1990s represented a period where the transformation from a labour-intensive model to a capital-intensive model was performed through technical change (Felker et al. 1999). Initiatives by foreign investors contributed to capital stock and transfer of innovative technologies, leading to radical change in the production methods of the manufacturing industry and to the success of neoliberal policies. Western capitalist development models inspired the development of the National Vision Policy (NVP), implemented in the period of 2000–2010. However, this policy attracted criticism that it was not consistent with local and cultural values. This plan intended to improve competitiveness in the economy, develop information- and technology-based production systems and attain high rate sustainable growth rates. Policies from this plan are still being implemented today.

The strategic policies as briefly outlined above played a monumental role in the improvement of foreign trade, industrialization, diversification in the agricultural sector, improvement of the modern agricultural production methods, improvement of the investment climate and environment, and of the productivity of human capital. The impacts of these strategic policies upon the development of the main sectors—including agriculture, industry, mining, services and construction—will now be analysed in separate headings.

Agricultural Sector

Agricultural sector plays an important role in the process of growth and development in developing countries like Malaysia. Despite that Malaysia is rapidly industrializing, agriculture is the second largest sector in the country. Its contribution to employment and to the provision of food makes it a strategically important sector (Murad et al. 2008). Due to the utilization of conventional agricultural production methods up to the 1980s, product diversity has become extremely poor and agricultural revenues have declined. In 1984, National Agricultural Policy (NAP) was implemented to contribute to the development of the sector and to improve the added value in its outcomes (Rahman 1998). The need for agricultural raw material has become imminent in the same period due to export-oriented industrialization efforts. The growing industrial production also made it imperative to have more agricultural outcomes. The plan directed the focus to agricultural production, diversification of new export products, and industrial production for provision of raw materials to the industrial sector. As part of the plan, additional incentives were also introduced (Drury 1998). The size of the agricultural lands was increased after implementing agricultural policies. Some improvement has also been observed in the production of agricultural crops for domestic markets. The second NAP, implemented in 1992, helped the transfer of government incentives to the producers in rural areas. In this period where new lands were offered for production of additional crops, research and development activities allowing use of new technologies in the production were also performed [139].

The Asian financial crisis in 1997 negatively affected the Malaysian economy; and the devaluation in the national currency after the crisis led to an increased cost of imported agricultural products. The growing interest in the sector made it necessary to develop agricultural policies (Selamat and Nasir 2013). After the crisis, measures were taken to develop agricultural policies for high productivity and sustainability. Attention was paid to organic agricultural production and exploring new export markets. As part of the national agricultural policy, some measures were also taken to reduce utilization of chemical substances in the agricultural production, to protect the environment, to improve the life standards of the producers, to reduce food import and to make positive contribution to the national economy (Murad et al. 2008). The use of some certain agricultural areas was particularly promoted, whereas lands with less productivity were allocated for alternative agricultural products (Rahman 1998).

Development of new strategies has become essential in the aftermath of 2010 due to the reduction of agricultural areas, lack of labour and increase in production costs; as a result of this, Fourth National Agricultural Policy was taken into implementation. As part of this policy, employment of more than 100,000 new jobs in rural areas and a production size of 15 billion USD by 2020 are being pursued (Dardak 2015).

Industrial Sector

The evolution of the industrial sector in the Malaysian economy can be analysed in six main periods: (*i*) the period of 1867–1957 where British ruled as colony; (*ii*) the period of 1957–1969 from independence through the start of class conflicts; (*iii*) the period of 1970–1980 where export-oriented industries were promoted; (*iv*) the period of 1980–1986 highlighting liberalization movements; (*v*) the period of 1987–1997 when the Asian crisis broke out and (*vi*) the period of 1997–2005 when the policies to restructure were implemented in the aftermath of the crisis (Kinuthia 2009).

In the colonial period, there was a lack of developed industry due to low-intensity industrial production. Afterwards, some mining industries made appearances in the late 1950s under the lead of Chinese and European investors. Demand for mine and raw materials declined significantly in the international markets during the Great Depression of 1929, negatively effecting production facilities and crop lands (Sukirno 2008). The war deeply affected all developed nations of Europe, which featured significant demand for raw materials in the aftermath. This led to an increased production in mining because of the growing demand in industrialized economies.

The industrialization policies started to change after the declaration of independence. The economic policies focused on import-substituted industrialization strategy, protectionist practices and policies of incentive for foreign investment and capital. The government—aware of the need for infrastructure capital for industrialization—paid attention to expanding the railway network and constructing new highways, ports and airports. To swiftly complete all of these infrastructures, domestic and foreign investments were supported by policies and incentives. However, by the 1970s, the rural segment still preserved its weight in the economy despite all of these efforts towards industrialization.

Malaysia's 5-year development plans have played an important role in the industrialization strategy of the country. The first plan implemented in the period of 1966–1970 was successful in raising the living standards of the people in rural areas and successfully dealt with ethnic conflicts. New investments were made in food and chemical industries in

1975 as part of this plan. Some progress was made in textile production and manufacturing of electronic devices in provinces such as Penang, Selangor and Malacca. This progress was in line with the incentives for the industrial sector through free trade areas in these provinces. Some arrangements were also made to provide funds for industrialization and infrastructure projects, and also to promote low-interest economic policies and tax exemptions (Webster 2014). The implementation of these policies raised the standards of the locals over time. However, despite visible progress, the political elite did not deem industrialization satisfactory in the 1980s.

In the period of 1985–1995, neoliberal policies increased in popularity within the industrial sector. Private sector actors started to pay greater attention to heavy industry and natural resources. Incentives for foreign direct investment attracted the attention of foreign investors, which improved the competitiveness in the international markets through technology transfer (Chandran et al. 2009). Special attention was given to the free industrial zone in the process of industrialization, as there are currently 19 free industrial zones in the country. Foreign trade transactions of the firms in these zones are exempted from customs, tariffs and fees. Instead, they are subjected to minimum rates. According to the legislation, at least 80*pct* of the production in the free industrial zones have to be exported because their production enjoys significant incentives. However, the economy was negatively affected by the Asian crisis during which the reserves of the Malaysian Central Bank (BNM) declined to 28 billion USD. The national currency dropped by 50*pct* in January 1998. The crisis led to the dramatic decline in the foreign portfolio investments. It also led to the collapse of the stock exchange markets and deterioration in the balance of payments. In response to the crisis, the government took some measures that included decreasing the public expenditures, postponing public investments, freezing new company partnerships, preventing inflow of short-term foreign funds and stopping local firms from making investments in foreign countries (Menon 2009). These measures yielded to positive results. By 2001, the industrial sector became the most prominent sector contributing to the economy. However, global developments such as the September 11 attacks, wars in Iraq and Afghanistan and the SARS disease negatively affected the growth in the early 2000s. Therefore, the government took action to respond to the declining private sector investments (Yusof 2008).

Following the political and economic developments during the Asian crisis, a new era began in Malaysia's industrialization strategy. In 2005, the government decided to emphasize technology and innovation and further implement the Ninth Development Plan. The plan mainly sought to support mid- and small-sized enterprises in the industrial sector, establish links with the global economy, discover resources for industrial growth, generate human capital for industrial and technological development and implement new incentives for high added-value production.

The industrialization strategies implemented over the last five decades have contributed to the development and improvement of subsectors including electronics, textile, chemical products, transportation devices, construction, machinery, optics and processes agricultural products. The development plans mainly sought to improve the private sector. However, public capital was an important contributor to the high added-value sectors including vessel construction, telecommunications, steel and plantation. As a result of these policies and efforts, more than 50*pct* of the global microchip production was performed in an organized production centre in Penang (NEAC 2010). The government has placed emphasis upon advanced technologies in recent years including manufacturing of LCD, plasma parts, petrochemicals, medicine, medical equipment, industrial machinery and other relevant elements.

Tourism and Construction Sectors

In developing countries, tourism contributes to employment and generates revenues for different chambers of the economy (Bhuiyan et al. 2013). This sector is the second driving force for growth in a developing global competition. According to the World Tourism Organization data, Malaysia ranked 14th in attracting the largest number of visitors in the world (Habibi et al. 2009). The first effort in promoting tourism in the country was the creation of Cultural Department in 1953, which was shortly after the independence. The government further implemented Tourism Development Corporation in 1972 and National Tourism Master Plan in 1975.

In 1972, The Malaysia Airlines Company was established to attract more visitors. In the same year, the government further developed and implemented policies to offer better services for international visitors, improve infrastructure services, enhance transportation opportunities, focus on the improvement of the southern and northern areas of the country and link the provinces. Also, NEP was implemented to make the local people active in the field of tourism. As a result of this policy, the number of people employed in this sector increased by 30*pct* in the 1980s. The National Tourism Master Plan (NTMP), announced in 1975, mainly sought to increase employment and revenues in selected areas and improve the tourism potential of the country under the NEP (Marzuki 2010). In the late 1980s, the government spent greater efforts to ensure improvement of the tourism sector and addressed the losses in national economy due to the global recession. In 1987, incentives were introduced through the establishment of the Ministry of Culture and Tourism. Tax exemption schemes were introduced for investments in different fields and branches of tourism (Mosbah and Abd al Khuja 2014).

Although the NTMP was partially successful, it failed to address the disparities among the regions. For this reason, new measures were taken in the 1990s to promote activities such as river tourism, fly drive vacation, ecotourism, culture tourism and recreational activities. These new incentives attracted more than 7 million visitors to the country (Marzuki 2010). The Malaysia Tourism Promotion Board (MTPB) was created in 1992 to promote Malaysia and its tourism potential worldwide, which established 29 offices in foreign countries (Awang and Abdul Aziz 2010). Malaysia appears to have a great tourism potential that involves natural attractions and wildlife. To use this potential, the government devised National Ecotourism Plan in 1996 under which infrastructure efforts were implemented throughout the country. Even though the Asian crisis negatively affected this sector, subsequent policies revived it. As part of tourism policies, the physical and cultural heritage has been preserved and special carnivals performed. Additionally, public awareness for tourism increased (Mosbah and Abd al Khuja 2014). As a result of these efforts, the number of tourists soared from 5.5 million in 1998 to 27.5 million in 2015.

The tourism sector was one of the elements of The Economic Transformation Program (TETP) introduced in 2010. As part of this program, some arrangements have been made to modernize the sector and align it with the goals of 2020. Future tourism policies focus on duty-free shopping, global biodiversity, improvement of cruise and golf tourism, hosting international meetings and organizations, improving spa industry and offering greater opportunities of accommodation, and greater emphasis upon Kuala Lumpur and Bukit Bintang as major tourism destinations (Mosbah and Abd al Khuja 2014). The government plans to triple currency revenues and increase the number of tourists to 36 million by 2020. It appears that the tourism policies have been successful in contributing to the development of this sector.

The construction sector falls behind the agricultural, industrial and service sectors in terms of contributing to the country's GDP. In the late 1960s, the government extended support for the construction sector in line with growing industrialization. On the other hand, construction activities were also funded by private bank loans in the same period. The government's contribution was mainly limited to the construction of low-budget projects for public servants and low-income groups. With the growing importance of oil and natural gas in the 1970s, the sector grew further through the construction of new facilities and buildings (Abdullah et al. 2010).

In the 1990s, larger funds were allocated for mega projects because of the positive contributions of the construction sector on employment, revenues and other sectors. Malaysian Construction Industry Development Board (MCIDB) was founded in 1994 to contribute to and modernize the construction sector. The mission and mandate of the board was to provide advising services for the sector and government regarding the industry. The mega projects and the policies devised under the coordination of the MCIDB contributed to the growth until the Asian economic crisis (Kamal et al. 2012). The crisis negatively affected the construction sector, which shrunk by 19.2*pct* in 1998. The general economic situation discouraged new investments and led to problems in funding infrastructure projects (Bhuiyan et al. 2013).

Due to the negative impacts of the fluctuations during the times of crisis, the construction sector faced serious challenges in 2000s when other sectors enjoyed some recovery.

In the period of 2006–2015, the Malaysian Construction Master Plan was devised to identify a strategic position on the sector, improve the knowledge and skills of the workforce, modernize the sector, implement new technologies and perform innovation works and policies (Kamal et al. 2012). This incentive helped the sector grow again. In order for Malaysia to attain its goal of becoming a developed country by 2020s, Malaysia needs to maintain an average annual growth rate of 6*pct* and perform structural transformation in the economy. Considering the positive contributions of the tourism and construction sectors to Malaysia's growth, policies that will contribute to the development of both sectors carries great importance for the attainment of the 2020 goals.

Scope of the Work

This study utilizes a regression model in order to identify the potential impact of the loans provided by CF and IF institutions in Malaysia on its GDP. The data on the variables applicable to Turkey (in Table 4.2) in the previous chapter has been compiled for Malaysia from the Bank Negara Malaysia and Department of Statistics Malaysia Official Portal for the quarters between 1997:1 and 2014:4. Seasonally adjusted logarithmic data have been used in this study for this purpose.

Empirical Evidence

Before the econometric analysis, the graphs of the variables were analysed and the correlation matrixes were created to evaluate the correlation between the loans offered by the CF and the IF institutions and the GDP on a sector basis.

A review of the correlation matrix in Table 5.1 reveals that there is a positive, significant and strong relation between loans offered by CF and the GDP for all sectors except the construction sector. The correlation between loans in the construction sector and the GDP is 36*pct*. Table 5.2, on the other hand, shows that there is a significant positive and moderate correlation between the loans offered by IF institutions and the GDP. Additionally, there is low correlation (7*pct*) between loans by IF for construction sector and the GDP.

As Tables (5.3, 5.4, 5.5, 5.6, 5.7) show, there is high level of correlation between the residuals of some sub-models and SUR models. In addition to OLS, these were utilized as an econometric estimation method.

Table 5.1 The matrix of correlation between the loans offered by CF on sector basis and the GDP

	lngdp	*lnagriculture*	*lnconstruction*	*lnmining*	*lnmanufacturing*	*lntourism*
lngdp	1.0000					
lnagriculture	0.9422	1.0000				
lnconstruction	0.3657	0.4418	1.0000			
lnmining	0.7788	0.8507	0.7558	1.0000		
lnmanufacturing	0.9060	0.9223	0.6326	0.9191	1.0000	
lntourism	0.9790	0.9340	0.5184	0.8433	0.9452	1.0000

Table 5.2 The matrix of correlation between the loans offered by IF institutions on sector basis and the GDP

	lngdp	*lnisagriculture*	*lnisconstruction*	*lnismining*	*lnismanufacturing*	*lnistourism*
lngdp	1.0000					
lnisagriculture	0.6924	1.0000				
lnisconstruction	0.0706	0.6397	1.0000			
lnismining	0.3231	0.7703	0.8738	1.0000		
lnismanufacturing	0.6511	0.9807	0.6767	0.8147	1.0000	
lnistourism	0.4496	0.8597	0.8909	0.8934	0.8977	1.0000

Table 5.3 Estimation of the relation between loans offered by CF and IF for construction sector and the GDP by reliance on SUR

lngdp		*lngdp*		
Constant	9.8564[a]	Constant	11.6008[a]	
lnconstruction	0.1696	lnisconstruction	0.0200	
R^2	0.0410	R^2	0.0037	
χ^2	2.01	χ^2	0.56	
Correlation matrix			$\hat{u}_t$	$\hat{v}_t$
		$\hat{u}_t$	1.0000	
		$\hat{v}_t$	0.9436	1.0000
Breusch Pagan LM test		64.133[a]		

Note [a]Denotes significance at the level of 1%

Table 5.4 Estimation of the relation between loans by CF and IF institutions for agricultural sector and GDP through OLS

lngdp		*lngdp*		
Constant	4.4914[a]	Constant		9.9836[a]
lnagriculture	0.6951[a]	lnisagriculture		0.2180[a]
R^2	0.8786	R^2		0.4735
F	504.84[a]	F		57.52[a]
Correlation matrix			$\hat{u}_t$	$\hat{v}_t$
		$\hat{u}_t$	1.0000	
		$\hat{v}_t$	0.4093	1.0000
Breusch Pagan LM test		12.063[a]		

Note [a]Denotes significance at the level of 1%

Table 5.5 Estimation of the relation between loans by CF and IF institutions for the manufacturing industry and the GDP through SUR

lngdp		*lngdp*		
Constant	−11.28[a]	Constant		9.4766[a]
lnmanufacturing	1.8936[a]	lnismanufacturing		0.2407[a]
R^2	0.7885	R^2		0.4162
χ^2	288.56[a]	χ^2		53.89[a]
Correlation matrix			$\hat{u}_t$	$\hat{v}_t$
		$\hat{u}_t$	1.0000	
		$\hat{v}_t$	0.7087	1.0000
Breusch Pagan LM test		36.163[a]		

Note [a]Denotes significance at the level of 1%

Table 5.6 Estimation of the relation between the loans by CF and IF institutions for tourism sector and the GDP through SUR

lngdp		*lngdp*		
Constant	1.0362[a]	Constant		9.7518[a]
lntourism	0.9101[a]	lnistourism		0.2180[a]
R^2	0.9558	R^2		0.2021
χ^2	1603.70[a]	χ^2		20.00[a]
Correlation matrix			$\hat{u}_t$	$\hat{v}_t$
		$\hat{u}_t$	1.0000	
		$\hat{v}_t$	0.2989	1.0000
Breusch Pagan LM test		6.434[b]		

Note [a]and [b]Denote significance at the levels of 1% and 5% respectively

Table 5.7 Estimation of the relation between CF and IF loans for mining sector and the GDP through OLS

lngdp		*lngdp*		
Constant	9.5181[a]	Constant		11.1599[a]
lnmining	0.2673[a]	lnismining		0.0972[a]
R^2	0.5366	R^2		0.1010
F	87.65[a]	F		21.19[a]
Correlation matrix			$\hat{u}_t$	$\hat{v}_t$
		$\hat{u}_t$	1.0000	
		$\hat{v}_t$	0.7935	1.0000
Breusch Pagan LM test		45.333[b]		

Note [a]and [b]Denote significance at the levels of 1% and 5% respectively

It appears that the correlation between the residuals of the regressions estimated between the loans offered by CF and IF institutions for construction sector and the GDP is 94*pct*. This indicates that the correlation, performed in reference to the Breusch Pagan LM test, is significant and the use of SUR model was appropriate. Because the elasticity coefficients were statistically insignificant based on the SUR model results, it could be argued that there is no impact on the GDP by the loans the CF and the IF institutions offer the construction sector.

It appears that the correlation between the residuals of the regressions estimated between the loans by CF and IF institutions for agricultural sector and the GDP is statistically significant (41*pct*). Every 1*pct* of increase in the loans offered by CF institutions for agricultural sector increases the GDP by 0.70*pct*, whereas the 1*pct* of the increase in the loans by IF institutions for agriculture sector increases the GDP by 0.22*pct*.

It appears that the correlation between the residuals of the regressions estimated between loans by CF and IF institutions for the agriculture sector and the GDP is statistically significant (71*pct*). According to the SUR models, every 1*pct* of increase in the loans by CF institutions for manufacturing industries increases the GDP by 1.89*pct*. Meanwhile, the 1*pct* of increase in the loans by IF institutions for manufacturing industries increases the GDP by 0.24*pct*.

It appears that the correlation between the residuals of regressions estimated between the CF and the IF loans for tourism sector and the GDP is statistically significant (30*pct*). According to the SUR results, the 1*pct* of increase in the loans by CF institutions for the tourism sector increases the GDP by 0.91*pct*. This becomes 0.22 for IF loans.

It appears that the correlation between the residuals of the regressions estimated between the CF and the IF loans for mining and the GDP is statistically significant (79*pct*). According to Breusch Pagan LM test result, the correlation is also significant, indicating that the utilization of the SUR model was appropriate. According to the SUR model results, 1*pct* of increase in the loans by CF institutions for the mining sector increases the GDP by 0.27*pct*, whereas this remains 0.10*pct* for IF loans.

References

Abdullah, F., V.C. Chai, and A. Annuar. 2010. An overview on the growth and development of the Malaysian construction industry. *Workshop on Construction Contract Management* 1 (12): 1–12.

Awang, K.W., and Y. Abdul Aziz. 2010. Tourism policy development: the Malaysian experience. *Journal of Tourism, Hospitality & Culinary Arts* 2 (2): 53–62.

Bank, W. 2004. *Countries: Malaysia overview*, 1–51. Malaysia: Economic Planning Unit Prime Ministerís Department Malaysia.

Bhuiyan, A.H., C. Siwar, and S.M. Ismail. 2013. Tourism development in Malaysia from the perspective of development plans. *Asian Social Science* 9 (9): 11–18.

Chandran, V.G.R., R. Rasiah, and P. Wad. 2009. *Malaysian manufacturing systems of innovation and internationalization of R&D*, 1–34. CBDS Working Paper Series.

Dardak, R.A. 2015. *Transformation of agricultural sector in Malaysia through agricultural policy*. [cited 2016]; Malaysian Agricultural Research and Development Institue. http://ap.fftc.agnet.org/ap_db.php?id=386.

Drury, B. 1998. The limits of conservative reform: Agricultural policy in Malaysia. *ASEAN Economic Bulletin* 4 (3): 287–301.

Felker, G., K.S. Jomo, and R. Rasiah, eds. 1999. Introduction. In *Industrial technology development in Malaysia: Industry and firm studies*, ed. R. Rasiah, and K.S. Jomo. Routledge: London.

Habibi, F., K.A. Rahim, and S. Ramchandran. 2009. Dynamic model for international tourism demand for Malaysia: Panel data evidence. *International Research Journal of Finance and Economics* 33 (1): 208–217.

Jomo, K.S. 2006. *Introduction. in Industrializing Malaysia: Policy, performance, prospects*, ed. K.S. Jomo, 1–14. London: Routledge.

Kamal, E.M., et al. 2012. The critical review on the Malaysian construction industry. *Journal of Economics and Sustainable Development* 3 (13): 80–87.

Kinuthia, B.K. 2009. Industrialization in Malaysia: Changing role of government and foreign firms. In *DEGIT, Dynamics, Economic Growth, and International Trade*, 1–36. Los Angles: DEGIT XIV Conference Proceedings.

Kogid, M., et al. 2010. Determinant factors of economic growth in Malaysia: Multivariate cointegration and causality analysis. *European Journal of Economics, Finance, and Administrative Sciences* 24 (24): 123–137.

Leong, H.K. 1992. Dynamics of policy-making in Malaysia: The formulation of the New Economic Policy and The National Development Policy. *Asian Journal of Public Administration* 14 (2): 204–227.

Marzuki, A. 2010. Tourism development in Malaysia. A review on federal government policies. *Theoretical and Empirical Researches in Urban Management* 8 (17): 86–96.

Menon, J. 2009. Macroeconomic management amid ethnic diversity: Fifty years of Malaysian experience. *Journal of Asian Economics* 20 (1): 25–33.

Milne, R.S. 1976. The politics of Malaysia's New Economy Policy. *Pacific Affairs* 49 (2): 235–262.

Mosbah, A., and M.S. Abd al Khuja. 2014. A review of tourism development in Malaysia. *European Journal of Business and Management* 6 (5): 1–9.

Murad, M.D., N.H.N. Mustapha, and C. Siwar. 2008. Review of Malaysian agricultural policies with regards to sustainability. *American Journal of Environmental Sciences* 4 (6): 608–614.

NEAC. 2010. New economic model for Malaysia. In *Part I: Strategic policy directions*, 1–193. Putrajaya, Malaysia: National Economic Advisory Council.

Rahman, A.A.A. 1998. Economic reforms and agricultural development in Malaysia. *ASEAN Economic Bulletin* 15 (1): 59–76.

Selamat, Z., and A.M. Nasir. 2013. Efficiency measurement of Malaysian agriculture firms. *International Journal of Trade, Economics and Finance* 4 (2): 79–85.

Subramaniam, R.K., M. Shaiban, and S.D.K. Suppiah. 2014. Growth opportunities and dividend policy: Some evidence on the role of ethnicity in an emerging economy. *Corporate Ownership & Control* 12 (1): 126–139.

Sukirno, S. 2008. *Growth and transformation of The Malaysian economy*. [cited 2016, 1 June 2016]. http://www.ekonomikerakyatan.ugm.ac.id/MyWeb/sembul20_1.htm.

Tan, E.C. 2014. Malaysia's economic growth and development: Challenges and the way forward. *The Singapore Economic Review* 59 (3): 1–17.

Webster, T.J. 2014. Malaysian economic development, leading industries and industrial clusters. *The Singapore Economic Review* 59 (5): 1–15.

Yusof, Z.A., and D. Bhattasali. 2008. *Economic growth and development in Malaysia: Policy making and leadership*, 3.

Authors' Biography

Dr. Mehmet Akyol is Assistant Professor of Economics. Dr. Akyol holds a PhD in Economics from the Istanbul University. He also teaches variety of courses including Introduction to Economics, Regional Economics and Globalization, and World Economics.

Dr. Ferda Yerdelen Tatoğlu is Associate Professor of Econometrics at Istanbul University. She was born and educated in Turkey, and served as visiting scholar at University of Leicester Department of Economics. Dr. Tatoğlu is most recently the author of "Introductory Econometrics A Modern Approach" (2013), "İleri Panel Veri Analizi" (2012), "Panel Veri Ekonometrisi"(2012), and many other research in economics and econometrics.

Dr. Murat Ustaoğlu is an Associate Professor of Islamic Economics. He was born in Turkey, and educated at the Ramapo College of New Jersey (B.A.) and the City University of New York (M.A.), and holds a Ph.D. degree in Economics. Dr. Ustaoğlu has worked at Bank of New York and JP Morgan Chase Bank in US. He is, most recently, co-author of Islamic Finance Alternatives for Emerging Economies (2014), Post-Conflict Syrian State and Nation Building (2015) and many research articles focusing Islamic Finance and Economics. Additionally, he teaches undergraduate and graduate level various courses in Economics.

CHAPTER 6

A Quantitative Reassessment of the Dual Banking–Growth Nexus in Indonesia: Comparative Analysis

Adem Levent, Murat Ustaoğlu and Ferda Yerdelen Tatoğlu

Abstract Economists who considered the growth performance in the past estimated that Indonesia would preserve its high growth rate performance in the long term. However, the national economy can be currently considered as a developing nation. In addition to public sources, domestic and foreign resources are also needed in the financing of high growth rate. Dual banking offers alternative financial capital opportunities for the developing Islamic countries. It could be argued that the IF serves as an alternative in Indonesia to finance investments. To better measure the probable impacts of the loans they offer upon the GDP, seemingly unrelated regression model has been utilized. A review of the both correlation matrix reveals that there is a strong positive relationship between the loans offered for the sectors and the GDP.

Keywords Indonesian economy · Development policies · Growth

A. Levent (✉) · M. Ustaoğlu · F.Y. Tatoğlu
Istanbul University, Istanbul, Turkey
e-mail: a.levent@alparslan.edu.trM. Ustaoğlu
e-mail: ustaoglu@istanbul.edu.tr

M. Ustaoğlu and A. İncekara (eds.), *Balancing Islamic and Conventional Banking for Economic Growth*, DOI 10.1007/978-3-319-59554-2_6

Introduction

The growth theory argues that a less developed economy will catch up with advanced economies in the world due to advantages including cheap labour, cheap raw material and productivity as long as the institutional structures and geographical barriers do not stop them (van Zanden and Marks 2012). On the other hand, a review of the history of economics reveals that the share of the less developed nations in the world economy is shrinking. Only a few exceptions in Southern Europe and the Far East can be cited. In other words, unlike theoretical assumptions, it is not always easy to break the chains of being a less developed economy. Developing countries have to consider domestic and global developments and implement economic policies decisively. Economic development is a process that requires decisiveness and discipline.

Some common problems have been observed in most Asian countries in the aftermath of the colonial era. Although economic policies were devised to be in line with the realities of the modern world, the traditional balance of power and cultural structures of the countries in the region were major obstacles to the proper implementation of these policies. The greatest obstacle for the governments was the difficulty to discipline the societies (Myrdal 2008). This requires a radical structural transformation in a wide range of issues, from education to health. A review of the brief history of Indonesia reveals that this can be a confirmed argument.

Indonesia has always been a popular destination for the Westerners. The Portuguese were the first to arrive in the Indonesian islands for trade purposes, followed by the Spaniards, British and the Dutch. Starting from the eighteenth century, the Dutch dominated the country and preserved their rule until the Japanese occupation during the Second World War. In 1945, independence was declared. However, official independence was gained in 1949, after four years of negotiations with the Netherlands.

After independence, economic policies seeking high growth rate were implemented. But transitioning from a less developed nation to developing nation requires time and patience. Considering scholars estimate that Indonesia will be one of the leading economies in its region, a relative success of these policies should be acknowledged. Economic policies, implemented by economists who received training and education in Western universities, have been aligned with the realities of the world for a successful structural transformation.

This study will briefly review the Indonesian economy and analyse the policies implemented to attain high growth rate. Subsequently, the support provided by CF and IF in different sectors including agriculture, mining, manufacturing, industry and tourism will be empirically analysed for a better understanding of the national dynamics for high growth rate.

Brief History of Indonesian Economy

Indonesia, the largest country in the Southeast Asia, is rich in natural resources and reserves, and thus has immense economic potential (Ismail and Masih 2015). However, a brief review of the economic history of the country reveals that this potential has not been used adequately. The practices and the policies implemented by the Dutch during the colonial era were cited as successful initiatives of colonialism. In the nineteenth century, the colonial government established a Culture System (CS) that lasted for four decades, allowing the exports of local products cropped by the domestic farmers in Java (Booth 1998). The Agrarian and Sugar Laws abolished the land tax levied by the colonial government for the exported goods in 1870. The CS system, which survived in the form of plantations, was successfully implemented until the 1860s. This system was replaced by the Dutch private initiatives after the growing influence of the free market system.

In the nineteenth century, the colonial policies raised controversies in the Netherlands. Liberal economists in Holland started to criticize the colonial system, arguing that the system failed to raise the standards of the local people. In 1901, new policies were devised to raise the living standards of the local people in the fields of health, education, public affairs and agriculture. This process, known as the reconstruction of the colonial system, is also called an ethnic policy. However, these changes did not lead to visible changes in the economy. Poverty and unfair income distribution remained a problem (De Silva and Sumarto 2014). The European and Dutch capital holders continued to remain influential in the economy. The most important domestic economic development in the early twentieth century was the transfer of Java to Sumatra. The Great Depression in 1929 was considered a major setback in the national economy as it seriously affected the domestic economy. After the crisis, Indonesia had to rely on its domestic market because its exports to European countries dropped significantly. This domestic market-oriented approach increased industrialization and agricultural production in Java area. The economy was placed under tight control after the Japanese invasion during the Second World War, which decreased growth and negatively affected trade. The declaration of independence became the first step towards improving the economic situation (Glassburner 2007; Dick 2002).

The national economy can be divided into three parts. The first is the parliamentary democracy period where political stability has not been attained due to coalition governments (1950–1957). This period can be characterized by economic instability where the Chinese entrepreneurs and other foreign actors mainly controlled the economy.

The second part is under Sukarno's leadership, known as guided economy or guided democracy between 1958 and 1965. According to Sukarno, Indonesian democracy should be original and unique and not be imported. This approach is called guided democracy (Kroef 1957). The government was involved in economic processes, whereas the private sector was not allowed to take bold actions. Additionally, central planning was implemented for economic development. Redfern (2010) also calls this policy-guided democracy because the Dutch firms were nationalized and a strong bans were introduced in this period. Even though production was weak, 70 *pct* of the national revenues were allocated to military expenditures. However, the social situation got worse. As a result of this, no effective development policy was implemented. The goal was to serve the leader of third world countries but Sukarno, who assumed crucial roles in the Non-Aligned Movement, failed (Yazid 2014; Rakove 2015). This guided democracy era ended in 1965 due to the limited flow of foreign capitals, high inflation rate and balance of payments deficits.

The third era started in 1966 and ended in 1997. In this period, Suharto implemented New Economic Policy (also known as New Order) where a number of economic and social reforms were implemented. The elitist administration under Suharto's leadership was called Weberian Patrimonialism, where a small group of elites held the power and the masses were sidelined (Crouch 1979). Additionally, some aspects of the market economy were also observed (Resosudarmo and Kuncoro 2006). The economic policies of the government were conducted by a small minority of economists and technicians known as Berkeley Mafia (Habir 1993). Some economic progress has been made in this period thanks to the increased foreign aid and private investments. As a result, Indonesia experienced an Asian Miracle (Yazid 2014; Balassa 1988). Symbolic appointments, contemporary justification and the careful exercise of power governed the economic policies under Suharto administration. The structure of the formal government institutions featured a hierarchical order including civilian bureaucracy, military forces and presidency.

In the New Order where the state played a huge role, the main characteristics of the economic policies included state-ownership and regulation, dependency upon foreign investments, and private economic initiatives by capital holders who had close relations with government circles (Liddle 1983). The flow of foreign capital generated out of the cooperation with the United States should also be underlined in the success of developmental policies. Unlike the Sukarno era, defense expenditures were reduced in this era and emphasis was placed upon some strategic sectors including agriculture, industry, mining, energy, communication and trade. This era represented the importance of cooperation with a superpower in regional development (Yazid 2014).

Most economic problems have been solved through rapid growth. Likewise, new policies also contributed to the solution of some social problems including unemployment, poverty and unfair income distribution (Suryadarma et al. 2013). One of the main features of New Order is the 5-year development plan devised for the national economy. Westerners contributed extensively to the first 5-year development plan of 1969–1974. More than half of the 3.5 billion USD was used to finance development expenditures. In the second 5-year plan, 35 *pct* of the 22 billion USD was used to finance development expenditures and foreign capital. Therefore, Westerners should be given credit in the success of the New Order that relied on foreign investment for development (Lipsky and Pura 1978).

Indonesia remained stable in economic terms in the period between 1965 and the Asian crisis under the Suharto administration. Despite lack of mature democratic culture and violations of human rights as well as widespread practices of nepotism, significant progress was made in industrialization. The government spent efforts to improve iron-steel, petrochemical and plastic industries under the Investment Policy List program in the early 1970s. State-owned enterprises (SOE) were also created to better use the oil revenues in industrial development. Capital flow in sectors where SOEs were influential was restricted (Sönmez 2001). The Asian crisis ended the Suharto era. Since the political administration also stepped down, this is called a double crisis (Booth 1998; Glassburner 2007; Dick 2002; Hill 2007).

Natural Resources

In terms of both geography and population, Indonesia is one of the largest countries in Southeast Asia. But Java and Sumatra islands are the main centres of economic activities. The climate is extremely rainy, being affected by Monsoon pattern. A part of the country consists of thick forests, whereas other parts are arid lands. Therefore, the territory is not suitable for agricultural activities. The land is cultivated in Sumatra and Borneo, but most agricultural activities are carried out in Java, as it is known for its huge population and productive lands (Booth 1998).

The development of industry in the country, which has rich sources of valuable mines and minerals, also depends on the trade of these sources. Oil export is the main activity in dealing with the balance of payments deficits. There is also production and extraction of some mines in small scales. Indonesia also has natural and manmade ports. Compared to Japan and India, it can be argued that Indonesia is richer in terms of natural resources (Glassburner 2007).

Human Resources

The long colonial past negatively affected the human capital of the country, which suffered from poverty and unfair income distribution in this era. Growth alleviated poverty, but a large number of people still lived under the poverty line. Poverty has been reduced by 34 *pct* in the period of 2002–2012, whereas the Gini coefficient has increased by 30 *pct* in the same period (De Silva and Sumarto 2014). The contribution of growth in addressing social and economic problems such as poverty and unfair income distribution is controversial.

Domestic migration and demographic imbalance were major problems in the country where two-thirds of the population reside in the Java Island (Glassburner 2007). The population growth caused enormous problems during the Suharto administration. Production level significantly dropped in traditional crops, leading to food scarcity. As a result of this problem, unemployment rate has also increased (Lipsky and Pura 1978). The ethnic structure of the population is an important factor in the management of human resources. There are mainly four different population types in the country: the Chinese minority, Hindus who live in the inlands, the Islamic community and tribal groups in the inner parts. Although the Chinese community became a strong actor after the Dutch companies, the community left in 1957 and lost their power under the Sukarno administration (Glassburner 2007).

Reforms Programmes

The data on growth indicates that the growth is stable but poverty and unfair income distribution remain major problems. A number of governments so far have focused on such problems as education, labour mobility, leading and lagging regions in their development programmes (De Silva and Sumarto 2014).

When Suharto came to power in 1966, a new programme was drafted to lay down the foundations of economic reforms. The economic policies devised by the technocrats who received training in the West were implemented for economic stability. The first measure economists took was to ensure flow of foreign capital and liberalize foreign trade. This measure worked well, reducing the inflation rate to a manageable level and improving the economic indicators. Given the success of these policies, it can be argued that Suharto era performed well in the economy (Resosudarmo and Kuncoro 2006).

The devaluation in November 1978 was the greatest economic challenge that the administration faced. In the aftermath of the devaluation, Bank Indonesia and the Ministry of Finance and Planning Commission took bold measures towards structural reforms and deregulation to address the balance of payment deficits (Booth 1998). The Suharto era economic reforms can be divided into two parts: reforms in the period of 1983–1991 and reforms in the period of 1994–1997. The goal of the two reform periods was to ensure that the economy no longer remains dependent upon the oil sector and the manufacturing and agriculture sectors become more effective. The reform policies worked out well. The reform package mainly included the following:

i. Increased financial liberalization to facilitate private investment and increased volume and size of banking activities.
ii. Growing investment and liberalization to have better economic productivity and to attract greater amount of foreign investment.
iii. Two devaluations in the 1980s to make the goods more competitive, except oil products.
iv. Tight monetary policies to preserve local currency inside the country.

v. New taxation regulations to increase public revenues which then increased the amount of public investments in education and health.

The goal of the 1994–1997 programme is different from that of the previous one. The government took bold decisions and implemented deregulation policies to increase the amount of foreign investments. Additionally, tariff changes were introduced in foreign trade. Nine strategic sectors were opened for foreign investments as part of this programme (Resosudarmo and Kuncoro 2006).

The economic policies implemented in the 1990s successfully balanced budget, liberalized currency regime, stabilized foreign capital movement and lowered inflation rate. Through a balanced budgetary policy, large investments were made. The government further implemented a number of reform packages. In June 1983, a deregulation programme involving new regulations in banking sector was implemented. Under the package, the heads of state were allowed to determine the interest rates proposed by Central Bank. The loan ceilings were made flexible for state banks.

A new tax law was introduced as part of the package implemented in the budgetary year of 1984–1985. This new law introduced three levels of tax rates and simplified the taxation system. Additional reforms were also introduced in the coming years in different sectors. A presidential directive reduced the powers of the regulative departments in 1985, which also transferred the powers of customs and taxation general directorate to a private Swiss company. The reform package of May 1986 involved foreign trade policies. This reform package also introduced the right to using imported raw materials for domestic firms. In September 1987, the non-tariff barriers were removed and the quotas and customs barriers were simplified. In October 1988, the financial deregulation policies were put under spotlight. New banks were allowed to be active in different fields (Medyawati et al. 2011). The November 1988 package focusing on trade, maritime, industry and agriculture sectors reduced non-tariff barriers. The maritime regulations were abolished. The December 1988 package opened the doors for foreign investors, whereas the July 1989 package included measures for greater involvement of SOEs in the economy (Sjahrir 1990; Booth 1986).

The Asian crisis that broke out in Thailand had a negative impact on the economic stability in Indonesia, thus, new economic reform packages were implemented under the IMF auspices in the period of 1998–2000. The crisis was felt deeply in 1998. The government had to apply to the IMF for financial supervision, pledging to follow a tight reform programme in return for an IMF loan of 12.3 billion USD within a period of 3 years. The first stage of the package was focused on the restructuring of the financial system. The banking system was redesigned, causing 16 banks to shut down because of their poor performance. The second stage sought to liberalize trade and foreign investments. Some restrictions were introduced to domestic trade. Despite all efforts, the IMF reform packages failed, as they were not sufficient to ensure improvement in economic performance. The government elected in the 1998 elections did not include technocrats. Due to the failure of these policies and student movements, the Suharto administration stepped down, being replaced by Habibie era (Resosudarmo and Kuncoro 2006). Growth after 1960 relied upon three main factors:

i. the economic recovery period that was successful through reforms as outlined above,
ii. the impact of utilizing high technology upon productivity based on structural transformation in the agricultural sector and
iii. the rapid growth of the manufacturing sector.

There is a bidirectional linkage between the second and third factors (Sjahrir et al. 1990). The growth that reduced poverty in the period of 1960–1990 was achieved thanks to contributions by agriculture and manufacturing industries. After Widodo was elected president in 2014, the economic policies entered a new phase. The government reduced the subsidies from 19.8 to 4 *pct* in the 2015 budget. The savings from this were channelled towards high-multiplier investments in infrastructure and it is expected that infrastructure improvement programme would drive GDP growth in the near-to-medium term (De Silva and Sumarto 2014).

Growth Dynamics

Thanks to the economic policies implemented decisively in the period of 1968–1981, the economy grew remarkably. However, the economy shrank by 4.5 *pct* after the global crisis. The Indonesian growth process is similar to those of many developed nations. Despite that it gives the impression of an industrialized country, Indonesia can be regarded as an agricultural nation because the share of the agricultural sector still remains larger (Booth 1986). After structural transformation, the share of agriculture started to decline; the share of the mining, manufacturing industry, public services and banking increased. According to the empirical findings by Medyawati et al. (2011), financial support by the finance sector makes significant contributions to growth and to the development of agriculture and manufacturing industry.

State is one of the important actors of sustainable development. Suharto's administration attempts to place emphasis upon growth and public institutions in economic development. This is viewed as the internal dynamic of the development. Suharto relied on the American support to resolve the economic issues and used the technocrats and experts who received education in the US. Therefore, it could be argued that the US has been the external dynamic of the development process. The success of the development and welfare policies, as well as improvement of the living standards was referred as the political goals of the government (Yazid 2014). It could be said that some progress has been made towards this end based on the estimates focusing on the growth potential of the country in the future. The Asian crisis affected the country, opening up a new era for the economy. The recovery process after the crisis can be divided into four stages:

i. maintenance of macroeconomic stability by reducing the public debts,
ii. adopting policies of liberalization in the economy,
iii. establishing political stability that was crucial to the implementation of the economic policies and
iv. attaining high growth rates through regional economic reforms.

Despite progress achieved in growth and welfare level, no plausible solution was offered for bribery and corruption (Resosudarmo and Kuncoro 2006). After the crisis, the new democratic regime made choices that weakened the central authority in the administration of the economy. The administration started to use new tools of economic policy through different institutions. Progress was achieved in growth and stability on a micro level and the environment of investment became more attractive (Hill 2007).

During the Asian crisis, it can be argued that the national economy was based on an outward model. Despite the crisis, the government did not abandon its liberalization policies. Protectionist policies were eased and made flexible. Despite domestic lobbying activities, the administration adhered to the policies of liberalization. These policies were mainly implemented to give the IMF a greater role in Indonesia's economy. These economic policies intended to reduce protectionism, establish the Ministry of Finance as the centre to solve crisis, and ensure the success of regional trade agreements and of the liberalization policies in the 1980s (Hill 2007). The government was able to deal with the 2008 global financial crisis thanks to the lessons learned from the Asian crisis. The economic policies devised by the administration are viewed as the main factor for this success. The financial sector, reregulated via different measures, was more resistant compared to the 1997 crisis. Additionally, the continued growth of China was a chance in the crisis because China was the largest market for the Indonesian goods and services (Hill 2007; Basri and Hill 2011; Basri and Sjamsu 2010).

According to the literature, there are numerous works focusing on the short- and long-term relationship between financial development and growth. Schumpeter (1911), McKinnon (1973) and Shaw (1973) focus on the direction of the relationship and lay down the theoretical foundations of the impact. In recent years, the number of empirical studies has increased. Calderon and Liu (2003), in their work involving 109 countries for the period of 1960–1994, conclude that financial development leads to growth. The Granger causality test shows that financial development effects growth, and growth effects financial development. They conclude that financial deepening contributes to growth mostly in developed nations and in long sampling intervals. Thus, financial development has huge impact on growth. The course of growth in Indonesian economy complies with this theory. Financial development and growth affect each other in a bidirectional fashion.

There are also works supporting causalities between growth and the development of financial markets. Arguably, there could be a bidirectional causality between financial markets and economic development. It is also possible to talk about a linear relationship between the evolution of financial markets and the loan rates for Indonesia (Raz 2013). In their study, Ismail and Masih (2015) empirically analysed the relationship between financial development and growth in Indonesia for the period of 1980–2013 by reliance on Autoregressive Distributed Lag (ARDL) model. They concluded that in the short and long run, financial development variables affect growth. For this reason, the policy makers who want to promote growth should design long-term policies.

On the other hand, despite theoretical conclusions on the causality between financial development and growth, findings in empirical works focusing on the period between 1997 and 2007 suggest that there is no strong causality (Majid 2007). Unlike other developing nations, when the financial sector became increasingly influential the main factors of growth were macroeconomic stability, international trade, efficiency of legal systems, religious diversities and progress in the field of economy.

Scope of the Work

This study relies on a seemingly unrelated regression model to investigate the impact of the loans offered by CF and IF institutions in Indonesia for the sectors upon the GDP. The data on the variables used for Indonesia was compiled from the Bank Indonesia and Statistics Indonesia database for the periods between 1997:1 and 2014:4.

Econometric Analysis

Before econometric analysis, the graphics of the variables have been analysed. Correlation matrixes have been formed separately for the correlation between the loans offered by the CF, IF and the GDP (Table 6.1).

A review of both correlation matrixes reveals that there is a strong relation between the loans and the GDP. In addition, the loans offered for the sectors are also correlation among themselves (Table 6.2).

Table 6.1 Correlation matrix between the loans offered by CF institutions and the GDP

	lngdp	*lnagriculture*	*lnconstruction*	*lnmining*	*lnmanufacturing*	*lntourism*
lngdp	1.0000					
lnagriculture	0.9794	1.0000				
lnconstruction	0.9925	0.9912	1.0000			
lnmining	0.9720	0.9692	0.9620	1.0000		
lnmanufacturing	0.9426	0.9864	0.9826	0.9295	1.0000	
lntourism	0.9773	0.9983	0.9924	0.9681	0.9873	1.0000

Table 6.2 Correlation matrix between loans offered by the IF and the GDP

	lngdp	*lnisagriculture*	*lnisconstruction*	*lnismining*	*lnismanufacturing*	*lnistourism*
lngdp	1.0000					
lnisagriculture	0.9606	1.0000				
lnisconstruction	0.9804	0.9864	1.0000			
lnismining	0.9239	0.9720	0.9568	1.0000		
lnismanufacturing	0.9210	0.9747	0.9640	0.9602	1.0000	
lnistourism	0.9654	0.9732	0.9752	0.9371	0.9714	1.0000

In addition, SUR has been used as a method of econometric estimation because of the strong correlations between the residuals of the submodels, as seen in Tables 6.3, 6.4, 6.5, 6.6 and 6.7.

It appears that the correlation between the loans offered by CF and IF institutions for the construction sector and the GDP are 81 *pct.* According to the Breusch Pagan LM test, the correlation is significant; indicating that utilization of SUR model was appropriate. A 1 *pct* of increase in the CF loans, as SUR model results suggest, increases the GDP by 0.74 *pct*, whereas a 1 *pct* of increase in the IF loans increases the GDP by 0.59 *pct.*

It appears that the correlation between the residuals of the regression between CF and IF loans in agriculture and the GDP is 77 *pct*, which is statistically significant. The SUR model results suggest that a 1 *pct* of

Table 6.3 Estimation of the relation between loans offered by CF and IF for construction sector and GDP via SUR

lngdp		*lngdp*		
Constant	5.1060[a]	Constant	8.5737[a]	
lnconstruction	0.7428[a]	lnisconstruction	0.5919[a]	
R^2	0.9435	R^2	0.9598	
χ^2	625.22[a]	χ^2	904.00[a]	
Correlation matrix			$\hat{u}_t$	$\hat{v}_t$
		$\hat{u}_t$	1.0000	
		$\hat{v}_t$	0.8096	1.0000
Breusch Pagan LM test		24.906[a]		

Note [a]Denotes significance at the level of 1%

Table 6.4 Estimation of the relation between the CF and the IF loans in agriculture and GDP via OLS

lngdp		*lngdp*		
Constant	5.9188[a]	Constant		9.8606[a]
lnagriculture	0.6607[a]	lnisagriculture		0.5055[a]
R^2	0.9574	R^2		0.9211
F	857.70[a]	F		435.70[a]
Correlation matrix			$\hat{u}_t$	$\hat{v}_t$
		$\hat{u}_t$	1.0000	
		$\hat{v}_t$	0.7679	1.0000
Breusch Pagan LM test		22.408[a]		

Note [a]Denotes significance at the level of 1%

Table 6.5 Estimation of the relation between CF and IF loans for manufacturing industry and GDP via SUR

lngdp		*lngdp*		
Constant	4.2590[a]	Constant		10.8059[a]
lnmanufacturing	0.7220[a]	lnismanufacturing		0.3758[a]
R^2	0.8774	R^2		0.8375
χ^2	269.27[a]	χ^2		188.67[a]
Correlation matrix			$\hat{u}_t$	$\hat{v}_t$
		$\hat{u}_t$	1.0000	
		$\hat{v}_t$	0.8631	1.0000
Breusch Pagan LM test		28.310[a]		

Note [a]Denotes significance at the level of 1%

Table 6.6 Estimation of the relation between CF and IF loans for tourism sector and the GDP via SUR

lngdp		*lngdp*		
Constant	4.5021[a]	Constant		9.1852[a]
lntourism	0.7012[a]	lnistourism		0.4998[a]
R^2	0.9537	R^2		0.9304
χ^2	773.98[a]	χ^2		497.25[a]
Correlation matrix			$\hat{u}_t$	$\hat{v}_t$
		$\hat{u}_t$	1.0000	
		$\hat{v}_t$	0.7102	1.0000
Breusch Pagan LM test		19.168[a]		

Note [a]Denote significance at the levels of 1%

Table 6.7 Estimation of the relation between CF and IF loans for mining sector and the GDP via OLS

lngdp		*lngdp*		
Constant	8.8520[a]	Constant		10.4285[a]
lnmining	0.4490[a]	lnismining		0.4557[a]
R^2	0.9848	R^2		0.8531
F	2676.33[a]	F		239.78[a]
Correlation matrix			$\hat{u}_t$	$\hat{v}_t$
		$\hat{u}_t$	1.0000	
		$\hat{v}_t$	−0.3687	1.0000
Breusch Pagan LM test		5.165[b]		

Note [a]and [b]Denote significance at the levels of 1% and 5% respectively increase in CF loans increases the GDP by 0.66 *pct*, whereas this is 0.50 *pct* for the IF loans.

It appears that the correlation between the residuals of the regressions between CF and IF loans for manufacturing industry and the GDP is 86 *pct*, which is statistically significant. According to the SUR model results, 1 *pct* of increase in the CF loans increases the GDP by 0.72 *pct*, whereas 1 *pct* of increase in IF loans increases GDP by 0.37 *pct* in the sector.

It appears that the correlation between the residuals of the regressions between CF and IF loans for tourism sector and the GDP is 71 *pct*, which is statistically significant. According to the SUR model results, 1 *pct* of increase in the CF loans for tourism increases the GDP by 0.70 *pct*, whereas 1 *pct* of increase in the loans by IF increases GDP by 0.50 *pct*.

It appears that the correlation between the residuals of the regressions between CF and IF loans and the GDP is 37 *pct* in the negative direction. This indicates that this correlation based on Breusch Pagan LM test is appropriate for the utilization of SUR model. According to the SUR model results, 1 *pct* of increase in the CF loans increases the GDP by 0.45 *pct*, whereas 1 *pct* of increase in the IF loans increases the GDP by 0.45 *pct* in the construction sector.

References

Balassa, B. 1988. The lessons of East Asian development: An overview. *Economic Development and Cultural Change* 36 (3): 273–290.

Basri, M., and H. Hill. 2011. Indonesian growth dynamics. *Asian Economic Policy Review* 6 (1): 90–107.

Basri, M., and R. Sjamsu. 2010. The Indonesian economy amidst the global crisis: Good policy and good luck. *ASEAN Economic Bulletin* 27 (1): 77–97.

Booth, A. 1986. Indonesia's economy: Performance and policy options in a post-OPEC world. *Southeast Asian Affairs* 11 (2): 122–136.

Booth, A. 1998. *The Indonesian economy in the nineteenth and twentieth centuries: A history of missed opportunities*. A Modern Economic History of Southeast Asia. London: Palgrave Macmillan.

Calderon, C., and L. Liu. 2003. The direction of causality between financial development and economic growth. *Journal of Development Economics* 72 (1): 321–334.

Crouch, H. 1979. Patrimonialism and military rule in Indonesia. *World Politics* 31 (4): 571–587.

De Silva, I., and S. Sumarto. 2014. Does economic growth really benefit the poor? Income distribution dynamics and the pro-poor growth in Indonesia. *Bulletin of Indonesian Economic Studies* 50 (2): 227–242.

Dick, H. 2002. The emergence of a national economy. In *The emergence of a national economy*, eds. H. Dick et al., 1–19. Australia: Allen & Unwin Press.
Glassburner, B. 2007. *The economy of Indonesia*. Selected Readings. Jakarta: Equinox Edition.
Grabowski, R. 2011. Indonesian economic development: Political economy of an effective state. *Journal of the Asia Pacific Economy* 16 (2): 241–253.
Habir, A.D. 1993. The emerging Indonesian managerial elite: Professionals amid patriarchs. *Southeast Asian Affairs* 11 (2): 161–182.
Hill, H. 2007. The Indonesian economy: Growth, crisis and recovery. *The Singapore Economic Review* 52 (2): 137–166.
Ismail, M.A.M., and M. Masih. 2015. *Causality between financial development and economic growth, and the Islamic finance imperative: A case study of Indonesia*, 1–19. Malaysia: INCEIF.
Kroef, J.M.v.d. 1957. Guided democracy in Indonesia. *Far Eastern Survey* 26 (8): 113–124.
Liddle, W. 1983. Polity and economy in Suharto's Indonesia. *Crossroads* 1 (3): 35–45.
Lipsky, S., and R. Pura. 1978. Indonesia: Testing time for the new order. *Foreign Affairs* 57 (1): 186–202.
Majid, M.S.A. 2007. Re-examining the finance-growth nexus empirical evidence from Indonesia. *Gadjah Mada International Journal of Business* 9 (2): 137–156.
McKinnon, R.A. 1973. *Money and capital in economic development*. Washington: Brookings Institution.
Medyawati, H., M. Yunanto, and G. University. 2011. Banking development, agriculture and manufacturing industry sector in economic growth in Indonesia: Do they influence? *International Journal of Trade, Economics and Finance* 2 (4): 312–317.
Myrdal, G. 2008. *Asian drama: An inquiry into the poverty of nations*. New York: Kalyani Publishers.
Rakove, R.B. 2015. The rise and fall of non-aligned mediation, 1961–1966. *The International History Review* 37 (5): 991–1013.
Raz, A.F. 2013. The nexus between bank credit development and economic growth in Indonesia. *DLSU Business & Economics Review* 23 (1): 93–104.
Redfern, W.A. 2010. Sukarno's guided democracy and the takeovers of foreign companies in Indonesia in the 1960s. In *Social science in history*. Ann Arbor: The University of Michigan.
Resosudarmo, B.P., and A. Kuncoro. 2006. The political economy of Indonesian economic reforms: 1983–2000. *Oxford Development Studies* 34 (3): 341–355.
Schumpeter, J.A. 1911. *The theory of economic development*. Cambridge: Harvard University Press.
Shaw, E.S. 1973. *Financial deepening in economic development*. London: Oxford University Press.

Sjahrir, S. 1990. The Indonesian economy facing the 1990s: Structural transformation and economic deregulation. *Southeast Asian Affairs* 117–131.

Sönmez, A. 2001. *Doğu Asya 'Mucizesi' ve Bunalımı, Türkiye İçin Dersler.* İstanbul Bilgi Üniversitesi Yayınları: İstanbul.

Suryadarma, D., A. Suryahad, and S. Sumarto. 2013. Sectoral growth and job creation: Evidence from Indonesia. *Journal of International Development* 25 (1): 549–561.

van Zanden, J.L., and D. Marks. 2012. *An economic history of Indonesia 1800–2010.* New York: Routledge.

Yazid, M.N.M. 2014. The Indonesian economic development after 1965: Developmental state, radical politics & regional cooperation. *SOP Transactions on Economic Research* 1 (3): 1–14.

Authors' Biography

Dr. Adem Levent is Assistant Professor of Economics. He holds a PhD in Economics from the Istanbul University, and his researches focused on institutional economics, political economy and Islamic Economy & Finance.

Dr. Murat Ustaoğlu is an Associate Professor of Islamic Economics. He was born in Turkey, and educated at the Ramapo College of New Jersey (B.A.) and the City University of New York (M.A.), and holds Ph.D. degree in Economics. Dr. Ustaoğlu has worked at Bank of New York and JP Morgan Chase Bank in US. He is, most recently, co-author of Islamic Finance Alternatives for Emerging Economies (2014), Post-Conflict Syrian State and Nation Building (2015) and many research articles focusing Islamic Finance and Economics. Additionally, he teaches undergraduate and graduate level various courses in Economics.

Dr. Ferda Yerdelen Tatoğlu is Associate Professor of Econometrics at Istanbul University. She was born and educated in Turkey, and served as visiting scholar at University of Leicester Department of Economics. Dr. Tatoğlu is most recently the author of "Introductory Econometrics A Modern Approach" (2013), "İleri Panel Veri Analizi" (2012), "Panel Veri Ekonometrisi"(2012), and many other research in economics and econometrics.

CHAPTER 7

Economic Development and Financing Growth in a Hydrocarbon Economy: Qatar

Murat Ustaoğlu, Selman Yılmaz and Ferda Yerdelen Tatoğlu

Abstract The appearance of the cities in the Gulf has been for a while marked by luxury cars, glorious shopping malls and magnificent buildings. However, these cities are no longer as vibrant as they used to be because of the sharp decline in the prices of the hydrocarbon products. The slowdown in growth has led to some structural issues in the Gulf nations. The governments in these countries have for the first time introduced the idea of taxes. The administrators, now aware of the structural problems, made efforts to ensure that the economy would not depend on hydrocarbon products alone. This part of the study is focused on the impact of financial sector loans in Qatar upon growth rate.

Keywords Gas and Oil sector · Economic growth · Islamic finance · Conventional finance

M. Ustaoğlu (✉) · S. Yılmaz · F.Y. Tatoğlu
Istanbul University, Istanbul, Turkey
e-mail: ustaoglu@istanbul.edu.tr

M. Ustaoğlu and A. İncekara (eds.), *Balancing Islamic and Conventional Banking for Economic Growth*, DOI 10.1007/978-3-319-59554-2_7

Introduction

Despite the fact that it is a small power, Qatar is able to use its soft power wisely and effectively as evidenced by its growing influence in regional affairs and integration with the world (Karabulut 2016). One of a few countries that enjoys a foreign trade surplus in the world, Qatar is a small monarchy of tribes with a population size of 2.2 million in the east of the Arabian Peninsula (State 2014). Despite the fact that Arabic is the official language, English is also widely spoken. Before the economic dynamics and policies, it is useful to briefly evaluate the type of government in this country.

Because the change of government is not done via elections, Qatar has experienced cases of power struggles, mostly coup attempts. The current head of state came to power as a result of a bloodless coup plot in 1995 against his father. The head of state assumes the titles of defense minister and commander in chief as well. Other official titles are also decided by the emir. The new constitution that entered into force in 2005 indicates that parts of the powers are delegated to the Advisory Council (*Majlis al Shura*). Two-thirds of the council is elected by the people, whereas the remaining members are appointed by the emir. But participation in the election generally remains low. The people appear to be indifferent to politics and political struggles (Erdem 2009).

Qatar does not impose sales tax, corporate tax and personal income tax because its export revenues are sufficient to cover the public spending. Such tax exemptions make investment attractive; as a result, it is able to attract huge amount of investments that contribute to economic development. However, hydrocarbon industry remains the key to the national economy. The rich sources have been wisely used by the administration. The revenues out of the marketing of these products have been used for the development projects. Owing to these projects, Qatar has become one of the fastest growing economies in the world. A country that was poor in terms of per capita income some decades ago, Qatar now ranks first in terms of per capita income in the world.

This part of the study focuses on the growth dynamics and then pays attention to the development of hydrocarbon industry. After a review of the financial sector and the policies implemented in the country, the impact of the loans offered by CF and IF upon growth will be empirically evaluated.

A Hydrocarbon Economy

In some cases, the economic performance of countries with rich natural resources may become poorer than that of countries with no significant natural resources. In a country where manufacturing industry is dependent upon one natural resource, the diversification of the industry will not become possible because of the high profits in that sector (Yardımcıoğlu and Gülmez 2013). The increased oil and natural gas prices lead to greater production in that industry and to less production of the conventional industrial products (Sözen et al. 2011). The non-renewable natural resource reserves serve as a major source of income which further leads to consumption. In this way, the monetary resources are allocated to the production of the goods that are not subject to foreign trade activities. When prices decline in spot markets, different problems may arise (Yardımcıoğlu and Gülmez 2013). This scenario can be basically seen as the brief economic history of some Gulf countries.

Brief History and Structural Changes

Most Gulf states depend upon oil and natural gas. However, despite the fact that they make large amounts of money out of hydrocarbon sales, most of these countries are unable to maintain a working and stable economic order. For instance, the total exports of Finland, a small country with 5 million people, perform better than the MENA countries with 400 million people in exports of non-oil products (Koçak 2011). The export performance is considered one of the key indicators of competitiveness and development for a country. Primary goods constituted 80 *pct* of the exports in developed economies five decades ago; today, manufactured goods constitute 80 *pct* of the exports (Gelb 2010). Similarly, 60 *pct* of export diversification has been observed in the last three decades (Chandra 2008; Morakabati et al. 2014). However, it is not possible to argue that the Gulf states with rich hydrocarbon reserves were successful in export diversification. For this reason, their economies are mostly based on the consumption supported by the state; a few others are even unable to do this, thus being ranked in the category of less developed nations struggling with major economic problems.

Aware of the economic deterioration, some Gulf countries took action to build an economy upon a strong basis. One of these countries was

Qatar, a fast-growing economy in the world (State 2014). A review of the macro indicators of the country reveals that it is strange to see that it is regarded as one of the emerging markets in the world by the IMF (Morakabati et al. 2014; Hoskisson et al. 2000). We need to take a look at the economic history of the country to answer the question as to why it still remains an emerging market even if it is a fast-growing economy with a major foreign trade surplus.[1]

The Gulf has been a subject of power struggle for a number of empires and states in the past including the Portuguese, Ottomans and British because of its strategic location and rich hydrocarbon resources. The Ottomans maintained the longest term of rule in the region, which ended in World War I as a result of Arab nationalism. Jasim bin Thani, known as the founder of Qatar who also served as district governor of the Ottoman Empire in the area in the period of 1878–1913, was a famous pearl trader with good connections with the British. Before he died, he recommended for good relations with the Ottoman Empire; however, his recommendation seems not to have been observed by his heirs (Kurşun 2004). With the end of the Ottoman rule, the British maintained domination. As a protectorate state, Britain signed agreements with Qatar, Bahrain and other similar small entities in the region. As part of this agreement of allegiance, the Gulf entities pledged not to make any agreement with third parties without notifying the British. The agreement remained in force up to the end of the British rule in the aftermath of World War II. However, despite the official end of the rule, the British remained influential in a number of states in the region (Erdem 2009). Economic development has not become an issue or concern because dependency upon the West did not allow the local rulers to devise a vision based on the realities of their own region.

Many things started to change after a visionary administration rose to power. The revenues out of the hydrocarbon sales produced welfare; but this was not sufficient for development. Aware of this, the administration made efforts towards a genuine structural transformation. The efforts paid well, making Qatar one of the most prosperous countries in the world (Gardner 2014). To better analyse the process of structural transformation, it is useful to take a look at the economic policies after World War II.

The Western world, in an attempt to prevent another global war, took measures in the post-World War II era. The measures were mostly part of a liberal agenda. To this end, the liberal West has established global economic institutions including IMF and World Bank as well as implementing policies of liberalization such as creation of GATT. The world economy has recovered as a result of these measures. In the same period, the monarchies in the Gulf relied on a hybrid model of protectionist and liberal policies. In some of them, the state has maintained a strong control in the economy and nationalized foreign companies. In addition, agricultural reform was introduced to address unproductive sectors (Devlin 2010). Egypt, Syria and Iraq, under the influence of Arab socialism, have relied on mostly protectionist policies with a strong state involvement. In the same period, some Gulf states including Qatar, on the other hand, have adopted policies towards strengthening the private sector up to the 1980s.

Since the 1980s, efforts were made towards liberalization in the economy. In a number of sectors, free enterprise and consumption was promoted through a variety of fiscal policies including attractive tax rates. For instance, a standard customs rate of 5 *pct* was applied to the goods traded with the EU and the US reinforced the open trade regime (Vellinga 2007). On the other hand, it is useful to recall that the regional realities determine the boundaries of the neoliberal policies. For instance, the state stayed involved in some fields considered vital for the sustainability and distribution of water resources, oil revenues and economic resources (Genç 2011). Similar intervention was also observed in monetary policies. To maintain price stability and low inflation rate, the local currency was pegged to the USD in 2002 (Vellinga 2007). Because the state was involved in the centre of economic policies, some economists hold that these countries cannot be regarded as liberal economies. Al-Khulaifi (2012), in his analysis of Qatar's growth performance, notes that the state has been the main drive behind the growth by making investments and spending out of the hydrocarbon revenues.

The nation has become significantly prosperous after the 1940s thanks to the oil revenues. Currently, the per capita income is 120 k USD (Da 2011). Qatar, rich of natural gas and oil, enjoys flexibility of making investments in different fields thanks to the attractive oil and natural gas revenues that constitute 70 *pct* of the total state revenues (Al-Khulaifi 2013). Investments made in the sector led to greater production capacity and larger amount of revenues. The national GDP rose from 302 million USD in 1970 to 212 billion USD in 2015. The annual growth rate was 16 *pct* in 2011. One of the reasons for the high growth rate is the rapid price increase in spot markets due to the growing demand in the world for hydrocarbon products (Yardımcıoğlu and Gülmez 2013). In an empirical work focusing on the trend in the countries in the region, Vellinga and Abdel (Vellinga 2007) note that a 1 *pct* increase in oil prices leads to 6 *pct* of increase in the welfare level. But inevitably, decline in the prices have great impact on a number of macro indicators. The same study further reveals that small changes in spot prices may become very influential on a number of macro variables including investment, economic capital, export, growth and current account balance. Increase in public revenues accelerated the industrialization process (Darrat and Al-Sowaidi 2010). In fact, the main goal in industrialization policies was to create a more diversified economy that would not be dependent upon hydrocarbon industry alone (Morakabati et al. 2014; Taner 2014). The government, as part of this objective, introduced some privileges for state-owned enterprises (SOE) and made investments in a number of sectors ranging from financial sector to telecommunications. QAFCO, founded in 1969 that started production in 1974, was the first industrial company in the country. Qatar Steel and QAFAC followed it, starting production in 1981 and 1999 respectively. Qatar Petroleum, owned by the state, was reorganized in 2002 and transferred some of the shares it held before to Industries Qatar (Da 2011). On the other hand, as part of the policies introduced to save the economy from dependency upon hydrocarbon sector, Qatar Science and Technology Park and Qatar Financial Center were created. Foreign investors were allowed to make production in these two free zones.

The results of the policies were pretty constructive and satisfactory. To make the growth sustainable, some major projects were introduced; as a result, Qatar has become one of the most attractive places of construction projects in the world. But the hydrocarbon sector remained the primary motor of development. According to the growth data announced by the Qatar Central Bank for the period of 2000–2011, the non-oil economy has grown 10 *pct* on an annual basis (İbrahim and Harrigan 2012). But this cannot be separated from the hydrocarbon industry because it was the investments that were made in construction, utilities and transportation projects to benefit from hydrocarbon sector that contributed extensively to the growth.

Development of Gas and Oil Sector

Some Gulf states realized that consumption economy based on non-renewable carbon resources will lead to significant problems in the long run because changes in the spot prices of the hydrocarbon sector may deeply affect the economy. For this reason, some of the countries in the region made attempts to prepare themselves for the post-oil era. Particularly the United Arab Emirates and Qatar made enormous progress on this matter.

Qatar, the biggest LNG exporter in the world, has been successful because of its decisive stance and serious financial investments. It maintained partnerships with international energy companies to export the natural gas in the form of LNG and implemented mega projects. The natural gas export constitutes 40 *pct* of the total exports. The annual LNG export will expectedly rise from 31 to 77 million tons. LNG facilities are the leading components of the manufacturing industry. Most of the gas reserves are to be found in North Field; the first gas fields were discovered in 1971. But they were only used for domestic purposes up to 1980s when the first liquefaction facility was established.

With the rise of the Asian countries, the spot prices increased along with the demand for energy. In parallel to these developments, export activities began. In 1996, the government started production in facilities at Ras Raffan; in 1997, a major agreement was concluded with a Japanese energy first. By this sales and purchase agreement, the first step was taken to enter the Far East gas market. Ibrahim and Harrigan (İbrahim and Harrigan 2012) note that despite the growing demand for energy, it is not easy to be competitive in a fairly volatile market. The most important disadvantage was that Qatar was not close to any major market. It had to compete with Malaysia, Indonesia and Brunei in Asian markets and with Algeria, Norway and Libya in the European market. The second physical disadvantage is the negative impact of being close to many unstable countries upon shipment activities. The solution developed for these problems is pretty simple: to make technological investments to reduce costs and build confidence for the markets. To implement these policies, a unique system involving gas production facilities and shipment ports was established. The performance in the recent years confirms the success of the system.

Investments in the gas sector were not limited to LNG. In 2011, production of commercial clean burning began in gas-to-liquid (GTLs) facilities. Currently, Qatar is exporter of both. But production and export of the GTL carries some hardships. The spot price generally remains low because there is no huge demand for it in the global market. In addition, the current technology used for its transportation is not so advanced, affecting the overall price and demand. Despite these difficulties, Qatar made investments in the field. As a result, it currently appears to be an important player that determines the price of this product in global markets (İbrahim and Harrigan 2012).

It can be argued that the oil production of Qatar is modest when compared to other Gulf states. The daily production of half million barrels in 1970s has been gradually reduced by almost half due to change of strategy in the 1990s. But the production has risen again within two decades as a result of the production-sharing agreement with international energy companies. Currently, daily oil production is around 700 k barrels.

Labour Market and Education Policy

Sustainable development requires qualified labour supply. For this reason, labour markets should be determined based on the needs of economic development. In the labour supply–demand relationship, maintenance of balance in terms of geographical representation and profession is essential. Given that the economic policies cannot be considered irrespective of the globalization process, the impact of the globalization upon labour markets depends on the liberalization of international trade, the internationalization of capital, technological transformation and changes in the macroeconomic policies (Koçak 2011). One of the cases where this factor is mostly visibly observed is Qatar because the population size falls short to sustain growth.

About 1.8 million people coming from Philippines, Nepal, India and others work in construction, health, service and energy sectors; this alone indicates that the migration policies have deeply affected the demographic structure and outlook in the country. The flexible migration policies contribute to the growth of the population size. As a result, currently, the local people constitute only one-tenth of the entire population. The locals generally work as high level managers, whereas Arabs from other countries are employed in banks, oil and gas facilities or in public offices (Koçak 2011).

To supply qualified labour for structural transformation in the economy, reform policies were introduced and investments were made in the field of education (Öztürkler 2012). In an attempt to ensure intellectual independence, Qatar University was recognized an autonomous status. The Supreme Education Council, founded in 2003, introduced a number of reforms to ensure that young people receive a high-quality education (İbrahim and Harrigan 2012). The measures worked effectively; currently, Qatar ranks one of the top countries with the highest employment rate among young people. The success in this matter raise hopes for the future as well.

Scope of the Work

This study seeks to evaluate the potential impacts of the loans offered by CF and IF institutions in Qatar upon GDP through utilization of seemingly unrelated regression (SUR) model.

Variables and Data

The data used in the model described below have been compiled from the Quarterly Statistical Bulletin at the Qatar Central Bank database for the period between 2006:1 and 2015:2. The data have been seasonally adjusted. The seasonally adjusted logarithmic data are used in the study Table 7.1.

Table 7.1 Variables used in the econometric analysis

Variable	*Meaning*
lngdp	GDP
lnpublic	Loans offered by conventional financial institutions to the public sector
lnrealestate	Loans offered by conventional financial institutions to the housing sector
lnconsump	Loans offered by conventional financial institutions to the general public for consumption
lntrade	Loans offered by conventional financial institutions for commercial purposes
lnindustry	Loans offered by conventional financial institutions to the manufacturing sector
lnservices	Loans offered by conventional financial institutions to the service sector
lnpublic	Loans offered by Islamic financial institutions to the public sector
lnrealestate	Loans offered by Islamic financial institutions to the housing sector
lnconsump	Loans offered by Islamic financial institutions to the people for consumption purposes
lntrade	Loans offered by Islamic financial institutions for commercial purposes
lnindustry	Loans offered by Islamic financial institutions to the manufacturing industry
lnservices	Loans offered by Islamic financial institutions to the service sector

Econometric Analysis

The graphs of the variables have been reviewed and correlation matrixes have been created to analyse the correlations between the loans offered by the CF and the IF institutions and the GDP Tables 7.2, 7.3.

A review of these two correlation matrixes reveals that there is positive and significant relation between the loans and the GDP. In addition, the loans offered for the sectors have high correlation among themselves as well. The Tables 7.4, 7.5, 7.6, 7.7, 7.8, 7.9 also reveals that there is high correlation between the residuals of some sub-models. For this reason, in addition to OLS, SUR model has been used as an econometric estimation method.

Table 7.2 The correlation matrix between the loans offered by CF institutions for the sectors and the GDP

	lngdp	*lnconsump*	*lnrealestate*	*lntrade*	*lnindustry*	*lnpublic*	*lnservices*
lngdp	1.0000						
lnconsump	0.8840	1.0000					
lnrealestate	0.9615	0.9624	1.0000				
lntrade	0.8919	0.9749	0.9702	1.0000			
lnindustry	0.8362	0.9141	0.9138	0.9421	1.0000		
lnpublic	0.9772	0.8643	0.9524	0.8857	0.7958	1.0000	
lnservices	0.8960	0.9442	0.9608	0.9674	0.9428	0.8663	1.0000

Table 7.3 The correlation matrix between the loans offered by IF institutions for the sectors and the GDP

	lngdp	*lnisconsump*	*lnisrealestate*	*lnistrade*	*lnisindustry*	*lnispublic*	*lnisser-vices*
lngdp	1.0000						
lniscon-sump	0.9598	1.0000					
lnisreal-estate	0.8924	0.8551	1.0000				
lnistrade	0.8955	0.8463	0.8541	1.0000			
lnisin-dustry	0.9564	0.9253	0.9173	0.9397	1.0000		
lnispublic	0.9507	0.9538	0.9151	0.8605	0.9412	1.0000	
lnisser-vices	0.8142	0.8464	0.8265	0.7321	0.7992	0.8718	1.0000

Table 7.4 SUR estimation of the relation between consumer loans offered by CF and IF institutions and the GDP

lngdp		*lngdp*		
Constant	6.0668[a]	Constant	10.0389[a]	
lnconsump	1.5091[a]	lnisconsump	0.5981[a]	
R^2	0.7716	R^2	0.7864	
χ^2	115.13[a]	χ^2	126.09[a]	
Correlation matrix			$\hat{u}_t$	$\hat{v}_t$
		$\hat{u}_t$	1.0000	
		$\hat{v}_t$	0.4713	1.0000
Breusch Pagan LM test		8.440[a]		

Note [a]Denotes significance at the level of 1%

Table 7.5 SUR estimation of the relation between housing loans by CF and IF institutions and the GDP

lngdp		*lngdp*		
Constant	9.2272[a]	Constant	10.5319[a]	
lnrealestate	0.6575[a]	lnrealestate	0.4257[a]	
R^2	0.9221	R^2	0.9188	
χ^2	436.43[a]	χ^2	416.31[a]	
Correlation matrix			$\hat{u}_t$	$\hat{v}_t$
		$\hat{u}_t$	1.0000	
		$\hat{v}_t$	0.6405	1.0000
Breusch Pagan LM test		15.588[a]		

Note [a]Denotes significance at the level of 1%

Table 7.6 OLS estimation of the relation between commercial loans by CF and IF institutions and the GDP

lngdp		*lngdp*		
Constant	9.2684[a]	Constant	10.4219[a]	
lngeneraltrade	0.8744[a]	lnisgeneraltrade	0.6872[a]	
R^2	0.7955	R^2	0.8020	
F	140.04[a]	F	145.80[a]	
Correlation matrix			$\hat{u}_t$	$\hat{v}_t$
		$\hat{u}_t$	1.0000	
		$\hat{v}_t$	0.2475	1.0000
Breusch Pagan LM test		2.327		

Note [a]Denotes significance at the level of 1%

Table 7.7 OLS estimation of the manufacturing industry loans by CF and IF institutions and the GDP

lngdp		*lngdp*		
Constant	10.1725[a]	Constant	11.7807[a]	
lnindustry	1.0228[a]	lnisindustry	0.3038[a]	
R^2	0.6992	R^2	0.9148	
F	83.68[a]	F	386.35[a]	
Correlation matrix			$\hat{u}_t$	$\hat{v}_t$
		$\hat{u}_t$	1.0000	
		$\hat{v}_t$	0.2394	1.0000
Breusch Pagan LM test		2.178		

Note [a]Denotes significance at the level of 1%

Table 7.8 OLS estimation of the relation between the public loans by CF and IF institutions and the GDP

lngdp		*lngdp*		
Constant	9.3034[a]	Constant	10.6699[a]	
lnpublic	0.5452[a]	lnispublic	0.3989[a]	
R^2	0.9548	R^2	0.9038	
F	761.07[a]	F	338.23[a]	
Correlation matrix			$\hat{u}_t$	$\hat{v}_t$
		$\hat{u}_t$	1.0000	
		$\hat{v}_t$	0.2407	1.0000
Breusch Pagan LM test		2.201		

Note [a]Denotes significance at the level of 1%

Table 7.9 SUR estimation of the relation between CF and IF loans for service sectors and the GDP

lngdp		*lngdp*		
Constant	10.1847[a]	Constant	11.2727[a]	
lnservices	0.5088[a]	lnisservices	0.2433[a]	
R^2	0.7733	R^2	0.6381	
χ^2	123.87[a]	χ^2	59.57[a]	
Correlation matrix			$\hat{u}_t$	$\hat{v}_t$
		$\hat{u}_t$	1.0000	
		$\hat{v}_t$	0.7317	1.0000
Breusch Pagan LM test		20.345[a]		

Note [a]Denotes significance at the level of 1%

It appears that the correlation between the residuals of the regressions between consumer loans by the CF and the IF institutions and the GDP is 47 *pct*, indicating that the correlation is significant and that use of the SUR model is appropriate. SUR model results indicate that a 1 *pct* increase of the loans by CF increases the GDP by 1.5 *pct*, whereas a 1 *pct* of increase in the IF loans increases the GDP by approximately 0.60 *pct*.

It appears that the correlation between residuals of the regressions between the housing loans by CF and IF institutions and the GDP is 64 *pct* and is statistically significant. The SUR model results indicate that a 1 *pct* of increase in the housing loans by the CF increases the GDP by approximately 0.66 *pct*, whereas a 1 *pct* increase in the housing loans by the IF institutions increases the GDP by 0.43 *pct* approximately.

It appears that the correlation between residuals of the regressions between the commercial loans by CF and IF institutions and the GDP is approximately 25 *pct* and is statistically insignificant. For this reason, use of OLS is appropriate in this analysis. The OLS model results indicate that a 1 *pct* of increase in the commercial loans by the CF increases the GDP by 0.87 *pct*, whereas a 1 *pct* increase in the commercial loans by the IF institutions increases the GDP by 0.69 *pct* approximately.

It appears that the correlation between residuals of the regressions between the manufacturing industry loans by CF and IF institutions and the GDP is approximately 24 *pct* and is statistically insignificant. The OLS model results indicate that a 1 *pct* of increase in the manufacturing industry loans by the CF increases the GDP by 1.02 *pct*, whereas a 1 *pct* increase in the manufacturing industry loans by the IF institutions increases the GDP by 0.30 *pct*.

It appears that the correlation between residuals of the regressions between the public loans by CF and IF institutions and the GDP is 24 *pct* and is statistically insignificant. The OLS model results indicate that a 1 *pct* of increase in the public loans by the CF increases the GDP by 0.55 *pct* approximately, whereas a 1 *pct* increase in the public loans by the IF institutions increases the GDP by approximately 0.40 *pct*.

It appears that the correlation between residuals of the regressions between the service sector loans by CF and IF institutions and the GDP is 73 *pct* and is statistically significant. The SUR model results indicate that a 1 *pct* of increase in the service sector loans by the CF increases the GDP by approximately 0.51 *pct*, whereas a 1 *pct* increase in the service sector loans by the IF institutions increases the GDP by 0.24 *pct*.

Note

1. According to Morakabati; technically, the reason is hidden on the definition of *advanced*, which includes health, education and diversity, as well as income. The HDI ranks Qatar 36th of 187 countries, which reflects the impressive growth of Qatar's HDI over the past two decades. It outperforms the Middle Eastern neighbours in the region in terms of its HDI score.

References

Al-Khulaifi, A.S. 2012. The relationship between government revenue and expenditure in Qatar: A cointegration and causality investigation. *International Journal of Economics and Finance* 4 (9): 142–149.

Al-Khulaifi, A.S. 2013. Exports and imports in Qatar: Evidence from cointegration and error correction model. *Asian Economic and Financial Review* 3 (9): 1122–1133.

Chandra, V., J. Boccardo, and I. Osorio. 2008. *A technological capability story behind exports of fish fillet and iPods*, 11. Washington, DC: World Bank.

Da, H. 2011. Qatar as an oil emerging market. *International Journal of Marketing Studies* 3 (3): 141–151.

Darrat, A.F., and S.S. Al-Sowaidi. 2010. Information technology, financial deepening and economic growth: Some evidence from a fast growing emerging economy. *Journal of Economics and International Finance* 2 (2): 28–35.

Devlin, J.C. 2010. *Challenges of economic development in the Middle East and North Africa region*. Hackensack, NJ: World Scientific.

Erdem, B.K. 2009. Orta doğu'da küçük ama önemli olabilmek: Katar örneği. *Akademik Orta Doğu* 4 (1): 27–59.

Gardner, A.M. 2014. *Urban growth and challenges to sustainable development in Doha*, 343–366. Tacoma: University of Puget Sound Sound Ideas.

Gelb, A. 2010. Economic diversification in resource rich countries. In *Natural resources, finance, and development: Confronting old and new challenges*. Algeria: Central Bank of Algeria IMF Institute of Algiers.

Genç, H. 2011. MENA bölgesinde uygulanan iktisat politikalarını belirlyen faktörler. In *Ortadoğu ve Kuzey Afrika Ülkelerinin Ekonomik Yapısı*, ed. H. Genç, and F. Sayım, 20–22. Istanbul: MKM Yayınları.

Hoskisson, R.E., et al. 2000. Strategy in emerging economies. *Academy of Management Journal* 43 (1): 249–267.

İbrahim, I., and F. Harrigan. 2012. Qatar's economy: Past, present and future. *QScience Connect* 9 (1): 1–24.

Karabulut, S. 2016. Katar'ın Türk ekonomisi ve dış politikasındaki yeri. *İstanbul Ticaret Üniversitesi Sosyal Bilimler Dergisi* 29 (2): 173–202.

Koçak, O., and E. Kavi. 2011. MENA bölgesinde emek piyasası ve istihdam yapısı. In *Ortadoğu ve Kuzey Afrika Ülkelerinin Ekonomik Yapısı*, ed.H. Genç and F. Sayım, 61–88. Istanbul: MKM Yayınları.

Kurşun, Z. 2004. *Basra Körfezi'nde Osmanlı-İngiliz Çekişmesi, Katar'da Osmanlılar 1871–1916*. Türk Tarih Kurumu Yayınları: Ankara.

Morakabati, Y., J. Beavis, and J. Fletcher. 2014. Planning for a Qatar without oil: Tourism and economic diversification, a battle of perceptions. *Tourism Planning and Development* 11 (4): 415–434.

Öztürkler, H. 2012. Katar ekonomisinin genel özellikleri. *Ortadoğu Analiz* 4 (45): 77–83.

Sözen, İ., K. Uslu, and V. Öngel. 2011. Ortadoğu ve Kuzey Afrika ülkelerinin rantiyeci ekonomi yapıları. *Istanbul Ticaret Üniversitesi Sosyal Bilimler Dergisi* 19 (10): 89–107.

State, U.D.O. (ed.) 2014. *Investment climate statement: Qatar*, 1–26. Washinton, DC: US Department of State.

Taner, A.C. 2014. *Basra Körfezi ülkeleri Kuveyt, Bahreyn, Irak, Umman, Katar, Suudi Arabistan, Birleşik Arap Emirlikleri hidrokarbon rezervleri zenginlikleri açmazı ve sarmalı*. 1–8.

Vellinga, N., and E. Abdel Galil. 2007. Trade liberalization and economic diversification: A dynamic CGE model for the economy of Qatar. *Studies of Business and Economics* 53 (1): 5–24.

Yardımcıoğlu, F., and A. Gülmez. 2013. OPEC ülkelerinde Hollanda Hastalığı: Petrol fiyatları ve ekonomik büyüme ilişkisinin ekonometrik bir analizi. *Sosyoekonomi* 19 (19): 117–141.

Authors' Biography

Dr. Murat Ustaoğlu is an Associate Professor of Islamic Economics. He was born in Turkey, and educated at the Ramapo College of New Jersey (B.A.) and the City University of New York (M.A.), and holds a Ph.D. degree in Economics. Dr. Ustaoğlu has worked at Bank of New York and JP Morgan Chase Bank in US. He is, most recently, co-author of Islamic Finance Alternatives for Emerging Economies (2014), Post-Conflict Syrian State and Nation Building (2015) and many research articles focusing Islamic Finance and Economics. Additionally, he teaches undergraduate and graduate level various courses in Economics.

Dr. Selman Yılmaz is Associate Professor of Economics at Istanbul University. He was born and educated in Turkey. Dr. Yılmaz holds PhD degree from Istanbul University, and teaches variety of courses at the department.

Dr. Ferda Yerdelen Tatoğlu is Associate Professor of Econometrics at Istanbul University. She was born and educated in Turkey, and served as visiting scholar at University of Leicester Department of Economics. Dr. Tatoğlu is most recently the author of "Introductory Econometrics A Modern Approach" (2013), "İleri Panel Veri Analizi" (2012), "Panel Veri Ekonometrisi"(2012), and many other research in economics and econometrics.

CHAPTER 8

Findings and Conclusion

Zeynep Karaçor and Murat Ustaoğlu

Abstract The main purpose of the Islamic economy is to build a new model to meet the minimum needs of human beings and to maintain social peace and cohesion. To this end, it seeks to ensure that wealth is not concentrated in the hands of a few privileged men and capital holders and to create a balanced economic system that observes the interests of both the individuals and the society. As a solution, Islam places emphasis upon charitable activities which can be promoted by an economy that generates welfare. However, compared to developed nations, most Islamic countries perform poorly in terms of generating welfare even though they produce raw materials. The Islamic countries seeking to narrow the gap in recent years, rely on realistic development policies and support the real sector.

Keywords Islamic finance · Conventional finance · Economic growth

---

M. Ustaoğlu (✉)
Istanbul University, Istanbul, Turkey
e-mail: ustaoglu@istanbul.edu.tr

Z. Karaçor
Selçuk University, Konya, Turkey

M. Ustaoğlu and A. İncekara (eds.), *Balancing Islamic and Conventional Banking for Economic Growth*, DOI 10.1007/978-3-319-59554-2_8

Findings and Conclusion

The advantages of IF, particularly when compared to its counterpart, include the partnership scheme where profit and loss are shared, asset-based financing, an investment approach that places emphasis upon the protection of the deposit holders and their savings and the effective use of the funds through transfer to the real sector. The developing Islamic economies have implemented some constructive policies to increase the share of IF in the fiscal system thanks to its positive contribution to the growth and development. Turkey, Malaysia, Indonesia and Qatar specifically have made efforts to this end.

But despite its growing popularity, IF has failed to offer solutions to some structural problems. For instance, pious Muslims are still suspicious of whether or not its activities comply with the main precepts of Islam which is the only religion that still upholds the prohibition of interest. A number of practices and activities of the IF that are trying to compete with the CF in global markets still raise some doubts. Muslim scholars have particularly discussed the linkage between these institutions and the practice of interest lending. It is not possible to offer a simple answer to these questions because it is hard to evaluate these institutions with reference to a single set of criteria.

Subsequent to the analysis of the Islamic Finance development issues, the theoretical infrastructure and foundation of each section has been explained in one section to avoid repetition before moving to the empirical analysis of the relationship between growth and finance. To better analyse the economic dynamics and growth policies of developing Islamic nations including Turkey, Malaysia, Indonesia and Qatar, the literature review was also presented in this section. The findings can be summarized as follows:

- The chapter summarizes the theoretical relationship between the financial sector and growth. It appears that there are three main approaches in the literature reviewing this relationship. One approach suggests that the financial sector supports growth, whereas the second argues that growth actually supports the development of financial sector. The most popular view today, on the other hand, suggests that there is a bidirectional relationship between financial sector and growth.

The section on empirical analysis starts with the review of the development process and economic policies in Turkey because it is the most developed economy that implements the Western development model among the Muslim majority countries. The political stability and economic policies pursued in the 2000s contributed to positive growth, making it one of the fastest growing economies in the world.

The rapidly developing real sector needs additional investments. The advantages of the dual banking system have been utilized to finance the investments. The financial methods of the two branches of this system seem to be similar; however, they are significantly differentiated in theory. The IF contributes to the growth of real economy thanks to the partnership model, risk sharing and asset-based financing. This makes the IF particularly stable and popular in times of crisis. The comparative empirical analysis in this section offers the following findings:

- The impact of the loans offered by the CF upon the GDP is most visible in the manufacturing industry, followed by agriculture, mining, tourism and construction industries.
- The impact of the loans offered by IF institutions upon the GDP is most visible in the mining industry, followed by agriculture, manufacturing, tourism and construction industries.

The second country analysed in empirical terms in Malaysia, an emerging economy in the Far East. The political development policies implemented decisively in its history played huge role in the attainment of the development and growth objectives. The growing welfare also helped in solving a number of social problems as well. The study starts with a brief analysis of the economic policies since the independence, followed by the empirical analysis of the contribution by CF and IF in meeting the financial needs of the real sector. The main findings out of the comparative analysis include the following:

- For the loans offered for the subsectors of the real sector, the impact of the loans by the CF upon the GDP is greater than the impact of the loans by the IF upon the GDP.
- The loans offered for the manufacturing industry for both types increase the GDP most. The impact of loans by CF upon the GDP is observed most in the manufacturing industry, followed by tourism, agriculture, mining and construction sectors.
- The impact of the loans by IF upon the GDP is observed most in the manufacturing industry, followed by agriculture, tourism and manufacturing industries.

Analysis of Malaysia is followed by the economic policies and growth process of another country in the region. Indonesia has followed an interesting trajectory of economic development after its independence. After a general review of its economic policies, the financing of the growth in Indonesia is analysed comparatively. The results of the analysis include the following findings:

- For loans offered to the subsectors of the real sector, the impact of the loans by CF upon the GDP is smaller than the impact of the loans by IF upon the GDP.
- Loans offered by both models for the construction industry increase the GDP most.
- The impact of the loans by the CF upon the GDP is observed most in the construction sector, followed by manufacturing, catering, agriculture and mining industries.
- The impact of the IF loans upon the GDP is observed most in the construction sector, followed by agriculture, catering, mining and manufacturing industry.

Initially, Egypt, United Arab Emirates, Qatar and Jordan were included in the work plan of this study for empirical analysis. However, there was no dataset for these countries, except Qatar. Therefore, only Qatar has been empirically analysed. Despite the fact that it is a small country, Qatar has attracted a great deal of attention in recent years thanks to its good performance in the management of its natural resources. Qatar has developed fast because of the proper investments in the hydrocarbon resources, resulting in the greatest amount of annual personal income. The economy generating this wealth is mostly based on the hydrocarbon industry. It has been observed in recent years that the works to diversify the economy and prepare the country for the post-oil age have paid off. When the largest six sectors of the economy have been comparatively analysed in terms of the sources of finances, the following findings can be presented:

- The impact of the loans by CF in Qatar upon the GDP is observed in consumer loans most, followed by loans for manufacturing industry, commercial loans, housing loans, public loans and loans for the service sector.

- The impact of the IF loans upon the GDP is most visible in the commercial loans, followed by consumer loans, mortgages, public loans, loans for manufacturing industry and for the service sector.

In the 2008 global crisis, the CF experienced serious problems in the global stage, whereas the IF performed well. Despite this relatively successful performance, the share of the IF institutions within the global financial sector is pretty small when compared to the CF. The share of IF in Malaysia is around 25*pct*, whereas it is 7*pct* in Turkey and Indonesia. But their share is growing. Given the structural differences and contributions to the economy, it is possible to understand why the IF is on the rise. The IF owes its popularity to risk management performance, financial model based on the principle of partnership, its ability to fund the real economy, refraining from uncertainty and speculative transactions and its contribution to the social cohesion and economy.

On the macro level, the reason for the rise of IF in Muslim majority countries can be attributed to its contribution to economic development and to the improvement of the real sector. It has to monitor the markets pretty closely because it has to fund the markets and take part in the investments as partners. For this reason, compared to its conventional counterpart, the IF is able to transfer funds more effectively. The empirical findings out of this comprehensive analysis suggest that IF is the most important alternative model for the global economy.

Authors' Biography

Dr. Zeynep Karaçor is Professor of Economics at Selçuk University. She holds a PhD in Economics, and, most recently, is the co-author of Macroeconomic Analysis, Financial Crisis, and many other research articles. Dr. Karaçor currently teaches various topics in economics, and the editor of various journals.

Dr. Murat Ustaoğlu is an Associate Professor of Islamic Economics. He was born in Turkey, and educated at the Ramapo College of New Jersey (B.A.) and the City University of New York (M.A.), and holds a Ph.D. degree in Economics. Dr. Ustaoğlu has worked at Bank of New York and JP Morgan Chase Bank in US. He is, most recently, co-author of Islamic Finance Alternatives for Emerging Economies (2014), Post-Conflict Syrian State and Nation Building (2015) and many research articles focusing Islamic Finance and Economics. Additionally, he teaches undergraduate and graduate level various courses in Economics.

Glossary of Arabic Terms

Emval	Assets
fa'ida	Benefit, utility
fatwa	Religious edict
fiqh	Islamic law, Islamic Jurisprudence
halal	Permissible
haram	Forbidden
ijara	Lease or hire contract
istisna'	future work contract
kiyemi	A legal term that refers to goods that are notunique
majlis al shura	Advisory council in Arabic culture
maal	Property/material wealth
misli	In fiqh, substituting (goods) without a difference that will affect the price
mudaraba	Profit sharing partnership
mugharasa	Variety of agricultural contract, joint ownership of land
murabaha	Profit added trust-based sales contract
musharakah	Joint venture
muzaraa	In fiqh, agricultural partnership
nama	Issued to represent the share of an incorporated partnership, written stock
qard	Loan
qard al ribavi	A type of loan which involves with interest
qard hassan	A loan extended on a goodwill basis (no interest)

M. Ustaoğlu and A. İncekara (eds.), *Balancing Islamic and Conventional Banking for Economic Growth*, DOI 10.1007/978-3-319-59554-2

qari	A person who memorizes whole Quran
re'sul-māl	Owner of capital
riba	Interest
riba al-fadl	Surplus
riba an-nasia	Deferment
sharia	Islamic law
tanzimat	The political reforms made in the ottoman state in 1839
tawarruq	A sales transaction that generates immediate cash
sadaqa	Alms
selem	future sale
sunnah	Prophet Muhammad's practices
ulama	Scholar
wadi'ah	trust contract
wakala	procuration contract
zahiri	Visible, virtual
zakah	Alms giving

Index

M. Ustaoğlu and A. İncekara (eds.), *Balancing Islamic and Conventional Banking for Economic Growth*, DOI 10.1007/978-3-319-59554-2

The manufacturer's authorised representative in the EU is Springer Nature Customer Service Centre GmbH, Europaplatz 3, 69115 Heidelberg, Germany. If you have any concerns regarding our products, please contact ProductSafety@springernature.com

Printed and bound by CPI Group (UK) Ltd, Croydon, CR0 4YY
25/09/2026
02222890-0013